New Policies, New Politics

New Policies, New Politics: Government's Response to Government's Growth

A Staff Paper by Lawrence D. Brown

THE BROOKINGS INSTITUTION
Washington, D.C.

1775 Massachusetts Avenue, N.W., Washington, D.C. 20036

Library of Congress Catalog Card Number 82-45979

ISBN 0-8157-1165-4

2 3 4 5 6 7 8 9

THE BROOKINGS INSTITUTION is an independent organization devoted to nonpartisan research, education, and publication in economics, government, foreign policy, and the social sciences generally. Its principal purposes are to aid in the development of sound public policies and to promote public understanding of issues of national importance.

The Institution was founded on December 8, 1927, to merge the activities of the Institute for Government Research, founded in 1916, the Institute of Economics, founded in 1922, and the Robert Brookings Graduate School of Economics and Government, founded in 1924.

The Board of Trustees is responsible for the general administration of the Institution, while the immediate direction of the policies, program, and staff is vested in the President, assisted by an advisory committee of the officers and staff. The by-laws of the Institution state: "It is the function of the Trustees to make possible the conduct of scientific research, and publication, under the most favorable conditions, and to safeguard the independence of the research staff in the pursuit of their studies and in the publication of the results of such studies. It is not a part of their function to determine, control, or influence the conduct of particular investigations or the conclusions reached."

The President bears final responsibility for the decision to publish a manuscript as a Brookings book. In reaching his judgment on the competence, accuracy, and objectivity of each study, the President is advised by the director of the appropriate research program and weighs the views of a panel of expert outside readers who report to him in confidence on the quality of the work. Publication of a work signifies that it is deemed a competent treatment worthy of public consideration but does not imply endorsement of conclusions or recommendations.

The Institution maintains its position of neutrality on issues of public policy in order to safeguard the intellectual freedom of the staff. Hence interpretations or conclusions in Brookings publications should be understood to be solely those of the authors and should not be attributed to the Institution, to its trustees, officers, or other staff members, or to the organizations that support its research.

Foreword

AMONG the most important political developments in the United States in the last two decades are growth in the scope and scale of the federal government's agenda and rising concern about the "new politics"—changes in the behavior and interactions of the president, Congress, bureaucracy, interest groups, and political parties. Some observers have found in the new politics evidence of disintegration and decay—an overcentralized executive, an activist but undisciplined Congress, an intrusive bureaucracy, the proliferation of single-issue special interest groups, and parties in decline. Thus even as the federal government has taken on new tasks, its institutional capability to fulfill them has been increasingly cast in doubt.

In this staff paper, Lawrence D. Brown, a senior fellow in the Brookings Governmental Studies program, argues that there is a causal connection between these two developments—that growth of the government agenda is itself one important source of the new politics. As policy commitments accumulate, Brown contends, the concerns of major ideological and partisan blocs tend to converge: liberals are obliged to address unintended, unwanted outcomes in the programs for which they fought, while conservatives work to contain the costs and improve the efficiency of programs they cannot (and often would not) undo. Both camps, then, increasingly shift attention from battles over "breakthroughs" that dominated politics in the past (proposals to add to the federal workload tasks previously left to the private sector or to subnational governments), and turn to means of rationalizing programs already in place (improving their efficiency, management, coherence, and coordination).

Reviewing the implications of the broadened policy domain for American political institutions, Brown points out that the new politics may be less a symptom of institutional decay than of adaptation. Nonetheless he cautions that the new preoccupation with making programs work while holding the size of the government agenda constant (or indeed even contracting it) may reduce the legitimacy of government in the eyes of critics who seek a more resolute and ideologically assertive style of politics.

Many persons offered useful comments on various drafts of this essay. Especially helpful were those of Giuliano Amato, Martha Derthick, James D. Farrell, Arthur Maass, James L. Sundquist, Donna D. Verdier, and James Q. Wilson. Secretarial assistance was provided by Radmila Nikolič, Joan P. Milan, and Pamela D. Harris. The manuscript was edited by Nancy D. Davidson. The views expressed here are the author's alone, and should not be ascribed to the trustees, officers, or other staff members of the Brookings Institution.

BRUCE K. MAC LAURY
President

November 1982
Washington, D.C.

New Policies, New Politics: Government's Response to Government's Growth

Policy determines politics.—Theodore J. Lowi*

New policies create a new politics.—E. E. Schattschneider**

MODELS of the behavior of political institutions generally depend heavily on prevailing images of the policy process. This dependence is not altogether comfortable, for no sooner do institutional models become settled and widely accepted than new policy patterns emerge to call them into question.

In the 1950s the inability of the federal government to discharge the agenda of the New Deal, repeatedly demonstrated in such fields as housing, education, civil rights, and health care, gave rise to an image of deadlocked institutions.[1] Frustrated or lethargic presidents skirmished with an internally divided Congress, while interest groups blocked action and the bureaucracy looked on helplessly. The deadlock image was abruptly shaken off in the 1960s when activist, self-confident presidents John F. Kennedy and Lyndon B. Johnson articulated a broad agenda of reform. This was especially true after large liberal Democratic majorities in Congress were elected in 1964 and Johnson worked cooperatively with an eager legislature and bureaucracy to enact new programs, while interest groups either joined in the game or were forced to the sidelines. Political observers came to be impressed above all by the dynamics of government growth: the models of pluralist democracy advanced by Dahl, Banfield, and others in the early 1960s were enriched by the incrementalist doctrines of Lindblom and

**Public Administration Review*, vol. 32 (July-August 1972), p. 229.

***Politics, Pressures, and the Tariff* (Prentice-Hall, 1935), p. 288.

1. James MacGregor Burns, *The Deadlock of Democracy: Four-Party Politics in America* (Prentice-Hall, 1963).

Wildavsky, which pictured a steady accumulation of additional resources on established bases.[2]

By the end of the 1960s many of the federal initiatives had gone seriously awry; pluralist democracy and incrementalism were now painted in the dark hues of Lowi's interest group liberalism and Allison's bureaucratic politics.[3] Trimming and recasting the federal agenda became the central policy concern. As the federal government struggled to check the consequences of its earlier activism, there arose a new and troubling image of political institutions in decline or decay. Although the new policies of governmental containment and constraint and the new politics of fragmentation were often perceived as having something to do with each other, the 1970s passed with surprisingly few efforts to build conceptual models that linked the properties of the new politics with those of the new policies.[4] This essay, which is essentially a rearrangement and synthesis of by now familiar themes, attempts to sketch some of these connections.

The New Politics

In the last decade it has come to be widely believed that the United States has developed a "new politics," meaning new relationships within and between the major institutions of government and between these institutions and their environment of political parties and groups. It is commonly argued too that these new politics are an important cause or symptom (or both) of a decline in political capacity, meaning the ability of the system to solve pressing policy problems. Explanations of these developments differ. Some attribute them to gradually evolving changes in social values and expectations that accompany rising incomes and education.

2. Robert A. Dahl, *Who Governs?* (Yale University Press, 1961); Dahl, *Pluralist Democracy in the United States* (Rand McNally, 1967); Edward C. Banfield, *Political Influence* (Free Press, 1961); Charles E. Lindblom, "The Science of 'Muddling Through,'" *Public Administration Review*, vol. 19 (Spring 1959), pp. 79–88; Lindblom, *The Intelligence of Democracy* (Free Press, 1965); and Aaron Wildavsky, *The Politics of the Budgetary Process* (Little, Brown, 1964).

3. Theodore J. Lowi, *The End of Liberalism* (Norton, 1969); and Graham Allison, "Conceptual Models and the Cuban Missile Crisis," *American Political Science Review*, vol. 63 (September 1969), pp. 689–718.

4. See, however, the important conceptual efforts of James Q. Wilson, which address many of the themes of this essay: "American Politics, Then and Now," *Commentary*, February 1979, pp. 39–46, and *American Government: Institutions and Policies* (D. C. Heath, 1980), especially chap. 23.

Others ascribe them to a recent series of unhappy accidents befalling American politics. A dangerous pattern of institutional decay set in amid the many crises that befell the United States in the 1960s and 1970s—a civil rights revolution, three major political assassinations, urban rioting, a protracted war in Vietnam, campus unrest and a noisy youth movement, a sexual revolution, the Watergate scandal, intermittent energy crises, and a high and unprecedented rate of inflation. Some fear that the decay has somehow grown chronic.

Whatever the explanation, concern runs high. Specifically, the nation is said to suffer simultaneously from a sharp rise in social and group demands, the worsening of major economic problems, and a steady decline in the capacity of the political system to set matters right. Government can no longer successfully manage social change and solve the problems of an advanced industrial democracy because even as the pace of change quickens and the severity of problems increases, government itself is breaking down. The evidence, say the critics, is everywhere: for example, government has proved unable to check double-digit inflation, except by inducing a deep recession and alarming unemployment levels; reliably reduce the nation's dependence on the oil-producing nations for energy supplies; contain medical, social security, and other program costs that are by its own admission uncontrollable; or eliminate costly and annoying governmental regulation. Yet at the same time that government demonstrates its incapacity to manage either the economy or its own undertakings, new demands from new and old groups agitated by the mobilizations of the past decade and a half add to its tasks. In the succinct words of an influential book entitled *The Crisis of Democracy*: "The demands on democratic government grow, while the capacity of democratic government stagnates."[5]

It is axiomatic that needs, wants, and problems are infinite and infinitely elastic. Nonetheless, if it is true that the responsiveness, competence, and legitimacy of the political system have changed decisively for the worse—if Sisyphus is really giving out—there is abundant cause for anxiety. The prospect invites attention to the new politics, or the "new American political system,"[6] and to the properties that have allegedly so enfeebled it.

Set one by another, the changes said to comprise the new politics make a

5. Michael J. Crozier, Samuel P. Huntington, and Joji Watanuki, *The Crisis of Democracy: Report on the Governability of Democracies to the Trilateral Commission* (New York University Press, 1975), p. 8.

6. This is the title of a recent compendium of essays. See Anthony King, ed., *The New American Political System* (Washington, D.C.: American Enterprise Institute for Public Policy Research, 1978).

weighty list indeed, and the pejoratives commonly attached to them are impressive and troubling. The list includes:

—loss of purpose ("passionless" politics);

—dominance of technique ("technocratic" politics);[7]

—growth of the executive office of the president, including White House staff ("overcentralization");

—growing bureaucratic role and presence ("overregulation");

—growing numbers of interest groups active in politics, especially single-issue groups ("interest group liberalism");

—congressional tendency to write highly detailed legislation ("inflexibility");

—greater legislative involvement in administrative details, especially by way of the legislative veto ("meddling");

—growth of congressional staffs, especially those serving committees ("new legislative bureaucracy");

—declining allegiance to and role of political parties ("collapse"); and

—growing role of the courts in policymaking ("judicial imperialism").

If these tendencies are growing simultaneously and if they deserve the pejoratives with which they are often labeled, the new U.S. political system may prove to be a very poor vehicle for system maintenance, conflict resolution, service delivery, or any other prominent function of the state.

The import and importance of this pessimistic prognosis are not obvious. An optimist may find that a little intellectual history casts them in a less alarmist light. Among any society's close and articulate observers, a disproportionate number are always highly impressed with the rapid pace and scope of social change around them. Those who offer the humdrum observation that today things look very much the way they did yesterday and will probably look much the same tomorrow have seldom won a great reputation for acumen. The analyst of penetration and vision—a Tocqueville, a Hegel, a Marx, a Schumpeter—is the one who discerns in the present the onward march of inevitable progress or decline and projects the causal path into the future, the one who makes sense of "the great changes and variations, beyond human imagining, which we have experienced and experience every day."[8] A plausible case can always be made that something important in society is fragmenting, collapsing, declining, or eroding. In a society

7. On "loss of purpose" and "dominance of technique" in modern politics, see Samuel H. Beer, *Modern Political Development* (Random House, 1974), p. 4.

8. Niccolò Machiavelli, *The Prince,* trans. George Bull (Middlesex, England: Penguin Books, 1978), p. 130.

like the United States, which enjoys mass education and literacy, a sizable issue-conscious college-educated stratum, and vigorous media, "the movement of the social system into self-consciousness"[9] is bound to be strong and the perceived pace of change rapid. The trick, of course, is to distinguish between deep-seated, deep-reaching change and spurious and epiphenomenal changes.

Ironically, social scientists, including political scientists, may not be among the most useful sources for interpreting the significance of change. Three aspects of the political science discipline in the United States account for this. First, political scientists tend to specialize in discrete institutions, becoming experts on the presidency, the Congress, the party system, and so on. Second, we tend to adopt, often implicitly, a functionalist framework, exploring and explaining the roles and functions of our preferred institution. Having identified these roles and functions to our satisfaction, we may be led too easily to the view that change is probably *dys*functional. Third, we political scientists sometimes are carried away by a public-spirited desire to be the first authority on the block to identify the latest threat to American democracy. As a result of these three tendencies, any number of changes—the entire list of elements of the new politics presented above, in fact—may be derided as grave threats to the roles and functions of time-tested institutions. Such judgments may be correct, of course; on the other hand, they may be too hasty, too deterministic, too impressed with the fragility of what has shown itself to be a very durable sociopolitical fabric, and liable to mistake adaptation for decline.

In sum, one may argue with equal plausibility that the new politics are a benign evolution of a fundamentally healthy political system or that they are both a dangerous symptom of and an independent contribution to an institutional decline that can only lead to malaise and worse. These arguments can be properly evaluated only after empirical examination of the leading features of the new politics and their sources.

The New Policies

The central fact of contemporary political life in the United States is the great recent growth in the scope and scale of the central governmental agenda. (*Scope* is defined here as the number of distinct activities govern-

9. Kenneth G. Boulding, quoted in Daniel P. Moynihan, *Maximum Feasible Misunderstanding* (Free Press, 1969), p. 164.

ment pursues. *Scale* means the number of citizens and groups these activities affect.)[10] This is hardly a novel observation; indeed, it is one that has been made of most Western postindustrial democracies with maturing welfare states.[11] But although political scientists devote much attention to explaining the growth of the governmental agenda, they too seldom turn the hypothesis around and consider that growth of the governmental agenda may itself explain political changes of highest importance. Policy, in a word, may "determine" politics. If so, it is possible that many features of the new politics, which are usually explained by reference either to nebulous changes in social values or to forces specific and endogenous to the institutions they afflict, may be traced to a common explanatory source: growth of government over time. This, at any rate, is the argument that will be developed here.[12]

No single-factor analysis—in this case policy as an explanation of changing institutional patterns and political styles—can hope to do justice

10. This definition, it should be noted, is neutral with respect to such measures of government growth as the percentage of the gross national product devoted to public spending or the size of the government service component of the domestic work force. These measures may be used to argue that government has become big or is not so very big at all, at one time or over time, as one prefers.

11. Writes Mexican poet Octavio Paz: "The state has been and is the dominating personality of our century. . . . Its reality is so enormous that it seems unreal: it is everywhere yet it has no face. We don't know what it is nor whom it is. . . . This is the crisis of the 20th century." (Alan Riding, "For Octavio Paz, a Solitude of His Own as a Political Rebel," *New York Times*, May 3, 1979.)

12. The argument is not, of course, that growth of government explains everything about the new politics. (The internal congressional reforms of the early and mid-1970s, for example, are probably to be explained largely in other terms.) It is merely that it explains important elements of some of them. And even when growth of government is a useful argument it is rarely a complete one. The point is simply that this is one important factor, one that would be at work even if others—changes in social values and institutional power balances, for instance—were held constant.

A full and rigorous discussion would tackle the question of whether policy as cause should be viewed as an intervening variable between such developments as affluence, postindustrialism, and political change, or as an autonomous independent variable in its own right. The correct answer is probably both, in some sense. These questions cannot be pursued here. For an early analysis of the impact of affluence on political behavior see Robert E. Lane, "The Politics of Consensus in an Age of Affluence," *American Political Science Review*, vol. 59 (December 1965), pp. 874–95. For a recent study contrasting the United States with West European nations see Ronald Inglehart, *The Silent Revolution: Changing Values and Political Styles Among Western Publics* (Princeton University Press, 1977). On postindustrial society see Daniel Bell, *The Coming of Post-industrial Society* (Basic Books, 1973), and Bell, *The Cultural Contradictions of Capitalism* (Basic Books, 1978), pt. 2; also Samuel P. Huntington, "Postindustrial Politics: How Benign Will It Be?" *Comparative Politics*, vol. 7 (January 1974), pp. 163–91.

to reality. Yet single-factor analyses are as much sought after and valued as they are simplistic, and not without reason: by purporting to explain a lot in terms of a little they offer generality (breadth) in social science propositions without sacrificing explanatory power (depth), thus reconciling two desirable qualities usually in tension.[13] Although such analyses seldom achieve refined and polished explanations, they may bring seemingly unconnected variables together in previously unrecognized ways and thus stimulate new efforts at explanation.

The argument may be outlined simply. As the governmental agenda grows larger in scope and scale, the following chain of events takes place. (1) New government programs produce new problems as well as accomplishments. (2) The new problems inspire political efforts ("rationalizing politics") to find policy solutions ("rationalizing policies"). (It should be noted that *rationalizing* is used here and throughout this essay as an adjective qualifying the nouns *politics* or *policies*. It denotes governmental efforts, whether successful or not, intended to make something—in this case, policies—more rational, that is, problem-free.) (3) These rationalizing politics grow increasingly prominent in the universe of political actions over time. (4) As they do so, they entail changes in political institutions and styles, changes that collectively constitute the new politics. (Thus the new politics are ultimately explained by growth of government.) (5) Finally, new politics generate new policies in their turn.

The term *rationalizing politics* as used here means an attempt made by government (though not necessarily initiated by it) to solve evident problems of existing government programs. It may therefore be distinguished from "breakthrough" politics—which may be defined as an effort (from outside government or within it) to get government involved in some activity hitherto performed privately or by another level of government, or to expand a governmental commitment.[14] In the United States, where the

13. George C. Homans, *The Nature of Social Science* (Harcourt, Brace and World, 1967), pp. 20–21, 83–87.

14. The pages that follow deal almost entirely with the federal government, the main source of breakthroughs and the major seat of responsibility for coping with their consequences. Tracing the implications of the argument for state and local governments would require a separate essay.

Some may protest that rationalizing politics are not a new political pattern but rather a variant of (or synonym for) such familiar processes as "political learning" (see Hugh Heclo, *Modern Social Politics in Britain and Sweden* [Yale University Press, 1974], chap. 6) and "incrementalism" (see Lindblom, "The Science of 'Muddling Through'"). After all, there is nothing new in the observation that government learns from and acts on its experience with existing programs or that it adds policy increments to reflect new political forces and accumu-

central government's role has grown slowly and late (in contrast to comparably developed European nations), many accounts of the domestic politics of policymaking are predicated on the breakthrough type of politics. In fact, the most familiar images of U.S. domestic politics portray what might be called a deadlock-breakthrough syndrome.

In this view, American pluralism or polyarchy locks a number of interested groups (organizations or other social formations) in combat over the proper scope of governmental activities. Each group applies resources as best suits its purposes to a range of decentralized organs of government—president, Congress, bureaucracy, judiciary, and (perhaps) party—and by complex bargaining among them these institutions reach an outcome that reflects the balance of power in society, that is, among activated groups. The outcome may well be an inability to act: that is, a group favoring inaction may persuade one of the decentralized institutions to withhold its consent, thereby producing deadlock. Indeed, this is a distinct possibility, because the combination of widely dispersed (pluralistic) political resources in society and widely dispersed (decentralized) powers in government tends to honor intensity of preferences. The structural bias of the system is toward inaction; a group seeking action must persuade the entire range of power-holding institutions to act, but one or a few intensely interested groups (veto groups) may block action by inducing a single major institution to refuse to act.[15]

lated experience. This is not the place for a detailed discussion about terminology, nor is one necessary. The contention here is not that rationalizing politics are unlearned or nonincremental (indeed the terms *political learning* and *incrementalism* are so broad that they seem to include most governmental behavior by definition, excluding only the random and the revolutionary), but rather that there is an important qualitative difference worth capturing with a distinct term. Whereas the political learning described by Heclo in Britain and Sweden mainly involved perceptions of the need to add new public programs to complement private or partial governmental efforts (the new programs being "breakthroughs" in the language used here), rationalizing politics aim to improve the workings of a troublesome set of established governmental programs whose scope and scale are, so to speak, held constant or even contracted. Whereas incrementalism has usually been taken to describe a slow but steady set of *additions* to the governmental agenda (though logically the increments need not be of "more"), rationalizing politics exhibit intense concern with changes in the *character* of existing programs, changes that may extend to what Paul R. Dommel calls "decrementalism" (*The Politics of Revenue Sharing* [Indiana University Press, 1974], p. 192). In short, the argument here is that although rationalizing politics may be viewed as a subtype of political learning or incrementalism, the subtype is sufficiently distinct to warrant a name of its own and sustained analysis in its own right.

15. Alexander Hamilton succinctly summarized the philosophy behind this conservative bias in his defense of the president's veto powers in *The Federalist*, no. 73: "Those who can properly estimate the mischiefs of that inconstancy and mutability in the laws, which form the

Action is therefore unlikely until a broad exercise in coalition and consensus building comes about through changes in attitudes, values, perceived needs, and (thereby) tastes for public action, which often follow a crisis such as a depression or war and are channeled into and expressed by means of election results. (If the changes are so large as to lead to a partisan realignment the election is dubbed "critical.") At this point, deadlock gives way to a breakthrough, a political explosion that adds a new commitment to the public agenda (or to a "reverse breakthrough," an effort to remove commitments from that agenda).

In sum, the key elements of the deadlock-breakthrough syndrome have generally been taken to be: multiple interest groups wielding widely dispersed political resources; decentralized political institutions, none of which can act effectively without bargaining for and securing the consent of others; a tendency for these dispersions of power to favor intensely felt preferences of groups hoping to veto new governmental actions; a government content to reflect the social balance of power; long stretches of policy deadlock yielding to gradually emerging consensus (often forged under the pressure of economic and social unrest), expressed in electoral coalitions and producing sudden, intermittent bursts of policymaking, that is, breakthroughs.

American politics in the last half-century have been shaped by the explosion and consolidation of three major breakthroughs, each comprising a host of public programs. The first was the commitment to new measures of public management of the economy by means of fiscal and monetary policy and new public efforts to secure the well-being of the disadvantaged. This commitment was initiated in the aftermath of the Great Depression and the critical election in 1932 that launched the New Deal and was extended after World War II by the Full Employment Act of 1946 and the creation of the Council of Economic Advisers. The second was the development of a major American military and diplomatic presence in international affairs, which began in World War II and was then reinforced by a series of crises, notably the Korean War, the cold war, the Sputnik surprise, the missile gap, and the Vietnam War. (These foreign policy breakthroughs do not and have never been thought to conform to the domestic deadlock-break-

greatest blemish in the character and genius of our governments . . . will consider every institution calculated to restrain the excess of law-making, and to keep things in the same state in which they happen to be at any given period, as much more likely to do good than harm; because it is favorable to greater stability in the system of legislation. The injury which may possibly be done by defeating a few good laws, will be amply compensated by the advantage of preventing a number of bad ones."

through syndrome, of course.) The third was a major expansion of the welfare state, which began in earnest in the New Deal, expanded slowly and incrementally in the 1950s, and accelerated in the Great Society and War on Poverty of the middle and late 1960s, triggered by the landslide presidential election of 1964.[16] The explosion and growth of these three breakthroughs—the managed economy, the warfare state, and the welfare state—have generated consequences that in turn have fueled rationalizing politics. The argument to follow deals mainly with the search for solutions to problems engendered by welfare state programs.

In the prevailing fascination with the conditions under which deadlocks give way to breakthroughs, it has gone largely unrecognized that over time a steady accumulation of policy breakthroughs may change the political system portrayed in the textbook model. Unfortunately, political scientists have tended to relegate the question of what happens after the legislative battle to the subdiscipline of administration and have then proceeded to spend much time debating whether the process is or is not, can or cannot be, "political" (the old school), or marveling over how complex a process administration (or "implementation") really is and wondering if the inevitable "bureaucratic politics" might not be "modeled." As a result, an important question—the impact of accumulating policy commitments on subsequent policy issues and on the political system itself—has been largely overlooked.

Whatever the merits of the deadlock-breakthrough syndrome as a description of the "old" politics, there are numerous and significant exceptions to it today. One major type of exception consists of breakthroughs devised within and adopted by government itself. The community action program and the general revenue sharing program, for example, appear to be breakthroughs produced by what Samuel H. Beer has called "public sector politics."[17]

Rationalizing policies, meaning measures adopted to cope with the consequences of previous government efforts, are a second and perhaps more common type of exception. These programs also frequently partake of public-sector politics. Public officials are often the programs' source of inspiration and main constituency.[18] Such programs come seemingly from no-

16. For documentation of the growth of the "defense shift" and "welfare shift" see Samuel P. Huntington, "The United States," in Crozier, Huntington, and Watanuki, *The Crisis of Democracy*, pp. 65–74.

17. Samuel H. Beer, "The Adoption of General Revenue Sharing: A Case Study in Public Sector Politics," *Public Policy*, vol. 24 (Spring 1976), pp. 127–95.

18. Such efforts do not come from this source alone, however. As explained below, interest

where and may enter the statute books not only without suffering prior deadlock but also with a suddenness that astonishes pontiffs of the politically feasible. In the 1960s and early 1970s, political scientists, heavily influenced by the conventional wisdom of the deadlock-breakthrough syndrome, were able to offer many reasons why it was not in the political cards for the federal government to regulate parts of the health care system and launch health maintenance organizations (HMOs), combine important programs of categorical aid into block grants, and deregulate the airline and trucking industries. That these initiatives were enacted not because of widespread constituency support, critical realignments, or party platforms, but instead largely as a result of government's own discontent with the workings of earlier governmental programs, suggests that there is a new and important political mode—rationalizing politics—which the deadlock-breakthrough syndrome does not describe well.

For purposes of this essay it will be convenient to assume that public programs are of two types only: breakthroughs and rationalizing programs. This is of course an oversimplification. In particular, one very important in-between type—the steady, incremental expansion of breakthrough programs over time—differs politically from both types postulated here.[19] However, the purpose of this essay is to highlight the character of rationalizing politics, not to offer a complete account of the politics of policy. Thus the benefit of economy of exposition may offset the cost in completeness.

Ends and Means

The dynamic of the connection between governmental growth and rationalizing politics may be described as follows. In the aftermath of a major breakthrough, both liberals (defined as those who support a larger central governmental role at the expense of the private sector and of subnational governments) and conservatives (those who oppose a larger central governmental role in favor of subnational governments or the private sector) are obliged to contemplate the new public program in a new light. Liberals who at first congratulated themselves on the latest triumph in committing the government to worthy ends come to recognize various unintended and un-

groups (public or private) disturbed by government programs are also an important source of rationalizing proposals.

19. On the distinction between "the adoption of a new policy and the amendment of an existing one," see James Q. Wilson, *Political Organizations* (New York: Basic Books, 1973), pp. 330–31.

desired consequences of their handiwork. Government's spending on the program may be unexpectedly high and seemingly uncontrollable, as in the case of medicare. Programs may be too complex and categorical to be administered successfully, as many urban programs of the Great Society were said to be. Scandals may break out, as they did in the implementation of important sections of the Housing and Urban Development Act of 1968. The original rationale for a program may come under persistent, persuasive attack, as did federal regulation of transportation in the 1960s and 1970s. Problems may arise sooner (within five years of enactment in the case of medicare, for example) or later (about forty years passed before "easy votes" on social security came to an end).[20] Whatever the reason and timing, policymakers who might prefer to be working for the next breakthrough feel compelled to pause, ponder over the maladies of their earlier efforts, and seek policy solutions to set matters right.

While liberals contemplate the need for repairs on their handiwork, conservatives, who earlier fought to keep the new commitment off the federal agenda altogether, come to recognize that the program they failed to block is here to stay. They are now concerned less about states' rights and the proper scope of government than about fiscal responsibility and control, administrative workability, honest and efficient administration, and a proper recognition of the prerogatives of the private sector and competition within a regulated framework in the programs they cannot hope to end; thus they join the liberals in seeking to shape programs in more rational directions.[21] A convergence results: both camps tend to agree that "the evils that worry us now spring directly from the good things we tried to do before,"[22] and both join in seeking means of rationalizing, managing, and

20. Martha Derthick, "How Easy Votes on Social Security Came to an End," *The Public Interest* (Winter 1979), pp. 94–105.

21. This may seem to be a strange description of American conservatives in the throes of the "Reagan revolution," but the following description of the new conservatives, by Senator Malcolm Wallop, Republican of Wyoming, shortly after Reagan's election, suggests that agenda convergence has not ended: "We emerged in an era where we began to tailor programs to the philosophies we were expressing. The older conservatives were there primarily as resisters to the liberal wave that started in the '30s. Theirs was essentially a defensive battle. Ours is an offensive battle, where we have complaints about the direction the country is going, but also positive alternatives to offer.

"Instead of moaning about the welfare state, [we are] aiming for funding mechanisms other than government to accomplish essentially the same goals—to lead the country through incentives rather than direct the country by fiat" (quoted in *Washington Post*, December 1, 1980).

22. Aaron Wildavsky, "Policy as Its Own Cause," in Wildavsky, *Speaking Truth to Power: The Art and Craft of Policy Analysis* (Little, Brown, 1979), p. 63.

reforming federal commitments. This process may be termed "agenda convergence."

Theses postulating the decline of ideology and the increase in convergence have been much debated, of course. Although these arguments usually point to broad socioeconomic and cultural trends as the engine of convergence, rather than to unexpected developments within the universe of public programs, the notion of agenda convergence is consistent with them. It would be more precise, however, to argue that as government grows ideology simultaneously declines, persists, and gets rechanneled. While ideological differences diminish within the sphere of rationalizing politics, they remain deeply felt and divisive in policy areas—energy, for instance—where a major breakthrough to governmental assumption of private functions has not taken place.

Moreover, *agenda* convergence should be distinguished from *program* convergence. That is, policymakers who agree on the need to rationalize public programs probably will not agree on the correct means of doing so. Ideological disagreements are rechanneled from questions about the role of government to ones bearing on the merits of the means of rationalization available to policymakers.[23]

Indeed, ideological disagreements about means (programs) tend to intensify even as ideological disputes about ends (the broad contours of the public agenda) lose force.[24] Distaste for the consequences of growth of

23. In *Political Control of the Economy* (Princeton University Press, 1978), Edward R. Tufte cites John Kessel's finding that in the social welfare field presidents' "modal activity," especially in their first term, is to respond to various segments of society by asking Congress to pass laws conferring benefits (p. 26). In consequence, transfer payments have become an increasingly important element in governmental spending (p. 58), a trend accentuated by the recurring stimuli of election years (p. 149). Although clear partisan divisions are to be found on these and other issues, there is also an important area of consensus: "a newly governing political party rarely throws out the major economic reforms initiated by the party it has displaced" (p. 89). Presumably these cumulative developments presuppose either a steadily growing economy, an increasing willingness among taxpayers to support governmental growth, or both. Given what has here been termed "agenda convergence" on such reforms, failure of these conditions may be expected to generate a demand for rationalization and a displacement of ideological dispute onto the programmatic means of reforming the reforms. The more that slowing governmental growth is viewed as critical, the more prominent disputes about means might be expected to become (p. 101).

24. Charles Anderson observes that "one might ask whether there is a tendency toward differentiation or convergence in the normative systems used in assessing public problems. On the one hand, in the last generation or so, there has been an overwhelming proliferation of new forms of policy expertise, social criticism, and perspectives on the problematic. Has public debate become more open and heterodox or has it become increasingly consensual and conventional?" ("The Logic of Public Problems: Evaluation in Comparative Policy Research," in

government generates increasing fascination with nongovernmental (or at any rate nonfederal) means of achieving given ends. Policy analyses that offer appealing private-sector alternatives therefore come into great demand. Demand generates an increased supply, and this greater supply in turn increases both the number of bearers of ingenious alternatives tugging at policymakers' sleeves and the sense that reform is in the air. As a practical matter economics offers the readiest, most systematic, and most easily grasped alternatives (as well as those most consistent with traditional American values), and so economists, especially conservative ones, loom ever larger in the councils of the rationalizers. Most of these policy analytic arguments and models are better dubbed "theoretical" than "ideological," but on occasion—the views of Ronald Reagan and Margaret Thatcher are cases in point—they may be so comprehensive and tenaciously held as to be ideologies. In rationalizing politics, ideology is continually reborn as hypothesis.

Among the numerous and diverse rationalizing strategies, seven are of major analytic importance. First, problems may be addressed by a governmental effort to create or alter *incentives*, usually in the form of monetary inducements. In the health field, for instance, government may attempt to control costs by building new cost-conscious organizations like HMOs to compete with fee-for-service providers, or it may make consumers bear a larger share of their health care bills in order to give them an incentive to seek care from less costly providers.

Second, the federal government may *decentralize* by entrusting to subnational governments activities it had been performing. The revenue sharing and block grant programs enacted in the 1970s and in 1981 were intended to invigorate the policymaking and administrative capacities of the states and localities, said to be inhibited and hamstrung by intrusive federal rules.

Third, government may *deregulate* by devolving its responsibilities to

Douglas E. Ashford, ed., *Comparing Public Policies: New Concepts and Methods* [Beverly Hills: Sage Publications, 1978], p. 26.) The implication of the distinctions between agenda and program convergence and between breakthrough and rationalizing politics is that the correct answer is "both," and indeed that the two developments go hand in hand.

Identifying the locus, force, and direction of ideology in society is obviously a very complex business, to which the rudimentary discussion offered here does not begin to do justice. For example, Felix Rohatyn's observation ("America in the 1980s," *The Economist*, September 19, 1981, p. 38) that "the voters in western democracies seem more and more willing to experiment ideologically in order to find satisfactory economic performance" suggests that voters may be more interested in and attracted to ideology even as they are less attached to and more pragmatic about it.

the private sector. Transportation deregulation was an effort to rationalize governmental arrangements that allegedly damaged the competitive vigor of the private sector. (If government followed the advice of some economists and exchanged regulation of air and water pollution for an approach based on pollution taxes or pollution rights, the result would fall under the headings of both deregulation and incentives.)

Fourth, government may *regulate*, that is, impose new legislative or administrative rules on previously unconstrained behavior. The distinction between regulatory breakthroughs and regulation as a rationalizing tool is often thin but not necessarily arbitrary. When government imposes new rules for one or more of the long list of classical reasons for regulation—to deal with natural monopolies, to avoid destructive competition, to contain spillovers, and so on—the policy may be counted as a breakthrough. Statutes establishing initial regulation of the trucking, drug, broadcast, airline, and other industries are cases in point. When such rules are imposed mainly to change the behavior of those participating in existing government programs, the policy may be called a rationalizing effort. For example, in 1972 amendments to the Social Security Act set up professional standards review organizations (PSROs) to monitor admissions to and lengths of stay in hospitals under the medicare and medicaid programs. Government-imposed price ceilings on natural gas are a breakthrough. Department of Energy regulations allocating fuel among sections of the country, within the framework of the government price ceilings, are a rationalizing policy. Changes in the social security program to cover new beneficiaries are a breakthrough. Increases in payroll taxes to keep the system solvent are a rationalizing policy.

Fifth, government may attempt to rationalize by setting up *planning* procedures. Faced with the problem of estimating costs and weighing competing claims for aid in one of the earliest breakthroughs, public works and water resource development programs, the government gradually developed elaborate procedures of benefit-cost analysis and related techniques. Persuaded that the accumulated force of foreign policy breakthroughs would demand a large military budget and more sophisticated strategic calculations than had been possible before, the Department of Defense in the 1960s developed systems analysis; planning, programming, and budgeting systems; and other planning approaches to rationalize the growing governmental and military commitment. Convinced that an enlarged system of domestic aid to cities could best be rationalized at the local level by a new forum for planning and citizen participation, the federal government set up the model cities program in 1966.

Sixth, government may *reorganize* programs or agencies. In 1974 it regrouped the regional medical, health planning, and Hill-Burton programs in a new bureau of planning and development, for instance. It has attempted to rationalize its energy efforts by creating a new Department of Energy and has combined its education programs in a new education department.

Seventh, government may *disengage* from a policy commitment on the grounds that the program in question was a mistake in the first place, has outlived its usefulness, has been poorly administered, is otherwise inefficient, or is simply too expensive. The extreme form of disengagement is to abolish a program, that is, to strike it from the agenda altogether. (This unusual fate recently befell the Law Enforcement Assistance Administration and the regional planning commission network, for example, and airline deregulation, which provides for the gradual demise of the Civil Aeronautics Board, may also be placed under this heading.) The usual method of disengagement, however, is the budget cut: the activity under scrutiny is left on the agenda, but its scope may be curtailed (to serving the "truly needy," for example) and it may be funded less generously than before.

It is unclear to what degree program convergence tends to accompany agenda convergence. In general, it may be surmised that conservatives have a special fondness for incentives, decentralization, deregulation, and disengagement, that liberals are readiest to resort to regulation and planning, and that reorganization shares the affection of both camps. Part of the intrigue of rationalizing politics, however, is that important people keep popping up on unexpected sides of issues and often adopt apparently inconsistent positions across issues. For example, some conservatives opposed revenue sharing on grounds of fiscal responsibility (the level of government that raises money should control its expenditure); and a strong Senate conservative, Wallace Bennett, Republican of Utah, was the main legislative supporter of the PSRO program. Equally interesting are the eclectics: for example, between 1971 and 1973 the Nixon administration recommended HMOs, pushed for revenue sharing, acceded to PSROs, imposed wage and price controls on the entire economy, and offered a wide range of reorganization schemes. Both Edward Kennedy, Democrat of Massachusetts, and Jimmy Carter strongly supported HMOs, and both simultaneously backed bills that would give the federal government broad new powers to regulate hospital charges and that would reduce dramatically the federal government's regulation of airlines. In sum, although rationalizing politics do not obliterate ideological and partisan differences, they dissolve and recombine some of them in new and unexpected ways. Faced with the realities of coping with governmental commitments, politicians who may divide clearly and distinctly along ideological and party lines on breakthrough questions adopt rationalizing positions that leave themselves and their followers unsure exactly what they, and their ideologies and parties, stand for.

As breakthroughs accumulate over time (they occur at different times in different policy areas according to the distinctive political coalitions at work),[25] policymakers spend increasing time and effort trying to rationalize their effects. Thus, rationalizing politics tend to gain prominence over time, sometimes at the expense of breakthroughs. (The continuing effort to get medical costs under control before enacting national health insurance is one case in point.) The two modes coexist, however, a fact that is as basic to understanding the workings of the contemporary U.S. political system as it is unsettling to those in search of a unified general theory of that system.

It is not assumed here that the growth of unexpected problems in breakthrough programs leads automatically to government efforts to rationalize. Such efforts are most likely when government itself feels a direct and tangible stake in change. The clearest cases in point are those in which the federal budget is afflicted by so-called uncontrollable spending, especially for social security, medical care, and social services. Rationalizing activity is also likely when government, although it bears no clear costs of its own from the status quo, sees a chance to offer the public direct material benefits from rationalizing. Thus, airline deregulation may have helped cut air fares—at least somewhat on some routes—for millions of consumers.

Rationalizing action is least likely when government's own stake in change is modest while the status quo finds strong support among important interest groups. Thus, price supports for tobacco and various other commodities have proceeded with relative stability despite long-standing critiques.[26]

25. Individual policy arenas may sustain more than one breakthrough. For example, medicare was a breakthrough; national health insurance would be another. Incremental extensions of social security payments would be better described as the consolidation or incremental expansion of a breakthrough, however. The difference is a matter of degree—more a continuum than a dichotomy—and cannot be captured precisely.

26. See "Farm Bill a Test of Reagan's Control of Spending," *National Journal*, October 31, 1981, pp. 1931, 1957; and Congressional Budget Office, *Reducing the Federal Deficit: Strategies and Options; A Report to the Senate and House Committees on the Budget—Part III*, February 1982, pp. 89–93.

Conversely, when government's own stake in change is small but an affected interest earnestly seeks it, rationalizing action is likely if countervailing interests in support of the status quo are weak. The block grants of the early 1970s offer particularly nice examples: the federal government followed the advice of the intergovernmental lobby to decategorize aid in the community development and manpower training fields, relatively new local functions where local bureaucracies enjoy little prestige for their professional skills and where employee associations are weak, but it declined to do so in the education and health fields, well-established local functions where professional public employees are numerous, self-conscious, and well organized. The argument here is not that rationalizing politics grow everywhere, but simply that they grow.

Institutional Consequences

Growth of the scope and scale of the governmental agenda produces certain policy consequences—unexpected problems in breakthrough programs—which in turn produce certain political consequences—"rationalizing" politics. Over time, the chain reaction leads to subtle but significant changes in the institutional framework of political behavior. These changes are evident in major governmental and political institutions: the presidency, Congress, the bureaucracy, interest groups, and political parties.

Presidency: Leadership Style

Growth of government changes both presidential behavior and the structure of the presidential office. The major behavioral change is that managing and repairing the breakthroughs of past administrations occupy a larger share of presidential time, over time.

Growth of government gets presidents involved, ambivalently but necessarily, in the search for managerial solutions to inherited problems that refuse to disappear. Feasible solutions are usually politically unappealing because they are arcane, do not confer new benefits or expand old ones on a large scale, and are not the stuff of which a historical reputation is made. The typical political response is predictable: presidents will pursue rationalizing strategies of necessity but try to cast them as breakthroughs whenever possible. As a result, the overpromising and overdramatizing that typically accompany breakthroughs in U.S. politics also accompany initiatives to manage their consequences. For example, the Nixon administration promised that HMOs would restore competition to the health care system, reorganize that system and its incentives, contain costs, and give doctors a motive to keep patients well instead of merely treating them once they were sick. That administration sold revenue sharing as a historic, principled dawning of a New Federalism, if not indeed a New American Revolution. (The Reagan administration now uses similar language in promoting block grants to the states.) The Carter administration advertised its urban program as a historic first, too: never before had the nation had a coordinated, coherent, overall urban policy scheme, albeit one that added few new funds and programs. The Reagan administration confidently invoked the hypotheses of supply side economics to support its prediction that a combination of tax cuts and budget cuts in social programs would simultaneously restore the nation's sluggish economy to good health, allow a vast increase in military spending, and balance the federal budget.

Presidents will also stalk opportunities for genuine breakthroughs, but over time new breakthroughs appear to be held hostage ever more tightly to those of the past. The pattern is evident in the Johnson, Nixon-Ford, and Carter administrations. The Johnson administration was one protracted breakthrough: program upon program was enacted with little attention to those "little" imperfections and inconsistencies of design that might prove troublesome in the future. As a result, the Nixon administration was obliged to pick up various pieces: What should be done about model cities, and, for that matter, the whole growing arsenal of urban and domestic grant-in-aid programs? How could rising medicare and medicaid costs be contained? What ought to be done about the hodgepodge of welfare programs? The policy responses—revenue sharing, HMOs, and the family assistance plan (FAP)—artfully blended the characteristics of breakthrough and rationalizing strategy. First proposed as an amendment to medicare and medicaid and then converted into a small program of grants and loans to entrepreneurs, HMOs were a cost containment effort that worked by means of a "new and different" approach to health care. The block grant programs of 1973 and 1974 decentralized several manpower training and urban aid programs, but also (along with the State and Local Fiscal Assistance Act of 1972, which created the general revenue sharing program) extended aid to many localities that had not received it before. The FAP proposal would have not only redesigned existing welfare programs but also would have extended aid to new beneficiaries. These programs, in short, might be dubbed "rationalizing breakthroughs."

The Johnson breakthroughs imposed a rationalizing task on the Nixon administration; the cumulative weight of the Johnson and Nixon efforts increased still more the rationalizing burdens on the Carter and Reagan presidencies and appears to have produced the purest versions of rationalizing politics yet seen in Washington. The Carter presidency made painfully clear the ambivalence and hesitation of politicians eager for breakthroughs but obliged to attend first to the nasty details of cleaning up after prior administrations. Carter's $500 billion budget for fiscal year 1979 stood almost $100 billion higher than outlays at the end of 1977, but about 90 percent of the increase met the rising cost of existing programs, leaving very little scope for breakthroughs.[27] That administration devoted much political capital to the fight for a hospital cost containment plan (a measure utterly without salient political benefits), but was unable to decide exactly what it ought to do about national health insurance. It promised to introduce coherence and coordination (two qualities in rather low political demand) into federal urban programs, but, much to the displeasure of its black and mayoral constituencies, could think of few new programs to propose. (After the vast enlargement of aid under the Nixon revenue sharing measures, new targeted aid for some areas could be purchased politically only by across-the-board side payments to all jurisdictions or by taking from some to give to others. The former course was too costly and the latter politically unacceptable.) Plans for welfare reform, as in the Nixon administration, foundered on the tension between the need to rationalize the status quo and the urge to confer new benefits.

The Reagan administration is a nearly pure case of rationalizing politics. (The point will be argued more fully below.) Promising to "get the federal government off the people's back," this administration has proposed no major breakthroughs at all (that is, although it has sought very large increases in defense spending, it has suggested no important additions to the welfare agenda of the federal government) and has thrown its energies entirely into altering the programmatic cast of the federal agenda by means of disengagement, incentives, and deregulation, all advertised as a stunning historical departure.

The disappearance (perhaps temporary) of the breakthrough-oriented presidency implies an important change in familiar conceptions of presi-

27. Hugh Heclo, "Issue Networks and the Executive Establishment," in King, *New American Political System*, p. 91.

dential leadership. In American politics, the breakthrough, in the form of transfer payments, new subsidies, or grants-in-aid that confer divisible benefits on specific groups or areas, has been a major means by which politicians win the approval of important groups and thereby maintain the support needed to govern effectively. If presidents fail to formulate breakthrough measures or fail to propose and guide them to legislative success, observers in interest groups, the media, and the academic community soon take a dim view of the administration's leadership. As Edward C. Banfield has emphasized, in American political culture a political leader does not just sit there, he does something.[28] But as a contemporary president pores over the intricacies of domestic policy, he learns at once that his hand is not entirely free. Previous commitments—medicare and social security, revenue sharing and block grants, the accumulating welfare programs of the 1960s, pollution standards for air and water, for example—must either be tolerated or changed as a precondition to "bold, innovative" action of his own. As policymakers sift through the many possible combinations of old and new, deadlines pass and breakthrough proposals fail to appear. Observers grow disenchanted first with the slow pace of progress and then with the modest scale of the proposal that finally emerges. This pattern afflicted the Carter administration's efforts in the health insurance, urban policy, welfare reform, and energy fields. Some of this hesitation may be explained by the peculiarities and political limitations of that administration itself. The argument offered here, however, suggests that much of it is probably explained by objective conditions.

In the old days, presidents made many of their proposals in their 100-day honeymoon period, and knew exactly where to place the blame for delay—on Congress or on some obstructive special interest such as the American Medical Association. (Alternatively, as in the Eisenhower administration, they declined to offer breakthrough proposals, stated their reasons, and then resisted legislative and interest group pressures to force their hand.) Even if breakthroughs succumbed to deadlock, therefore, presidents discharged the obligations of strong presidential leadership.[29]

28. Edward C. Banfield, *The Unheavenly City Revisited* (Little, Brown, 1974), pp. 273–74.

29. Though Eisenhower's efforts to resist breakthroughs have seldom won him credit for strong presidential leadership, his political sagacity has begun to be rated more highly of late. As Fred Greenstein, the leading revisionist, observes, "As Eisenhower came to be more and more aware that even a conservative who wished to put curbs on policy innovation needed effective representation of his views to Congress," his White House staff became "increasingly systematic in its efforts to advance the President's program." "Change and Continuity in the Modern Presidency," in King, *New American Political System*, p. 59.

Under the conditions of rationalizing politics, by contrast, it may become clear early in an administration that the incumbent did not fully understand the implications of his campaign promises, that a fundamental barrier to action is the administration's inability to make up its own mind, or that, given the accumulation of prior commitments, any feasible change may make matters worse, not better, on the whole. In short, as breakthrough opportunities dwindle in number and in scope, the impatience and disaffection of interest group constituencies and attentive elites mount. Presidents appear weaker sooner.

The growing prominence of rationalizing politics and the declining opportunities for breakthroughs change the complexion and tone of national politics. Rationalizing politics tend to be arcane, complex, bloodless, managerial, technocratic, prudent, reasonable—in short, not much fun for people bent on doing great things on a grand scale.[30] The Carter administration was perhaps the first in which rationalizing politics overtook and overwhelmed breakthrough politics.

Modest efforts to recast the governmental agenda and to slow its growth, as in the Carter administration, are a natural first step at rationalizing, but the powerful, self-sustaining forces of governmental growth, embedded deep in statutory design and daily politics, may give such measures the appearance of being too little, too late. Growing and extreme discontent with government may therefore invite more stringent strategies—concerted attacks on government itself and efforts not merely to constrain its growth but to shrink its agenda sharply and quickly. This is the limiting case of rationalizing politics, where such efforts shade, so to speak, into

30. William Glaser's discussion of the politics of health cost control in Western democracies captures the character of rationalizing politics nicely: "These were intricate problems of budgeting and setting rates for organizations (especially for hospitals) rather than price controls over doctors. Therefore, these did not involve highly personalized struggles between a few glamorous leaders of government (such as Aneurin Bevan, Lyndon Johnson, and Charles de Gaulle) and the leaders of the medical association. The struggles became bureaucratic exchanges among civil servants, finance officers, and auditors, with policies approved by political leaders. Within every government, policy was set and implemented by constant interagency communication."

In Canada, Glaser notes, cost control has become "a struggle between bright young econometricians, without a place for spell-binding political orators. So much of Canadian governmental decision-making has come to revolve around fiscal federalism, that the principal politicians in Ottawa and most provinces have become transformed into intelligent advocates of economic briefs." "Health Politics—Lessons from Abroad," in Theodor J. Litman and Leonard S. Robins, eds., *Health Politics, Policy and the Public Interest* (Wiley, forthcoming).

"reverse breakthroughs," and fundamental ideological disagreements about the ends of government reappear.

This strategy, illustrated by the Reagan administration, aims to make a virtue of necessity. Instead of talking blandly about sorting out governmental from private and central from subnational functions, as did the Nixon administration, and instead of allowing technical detail to sap political conviction and block communication, as did the Carter administration, Reagan has proclaimed that government itself is the main source of the nation's ills and has fervently endorsed rationalizing strategies as the road to economic and social recovery. The administration has substituted for technical complexity an all-embracing ideology combining elements of old-fashioned laissez-faire dogma with more recent supply side economics to generate a coherent (though implausible) set of programs communicated in language reverberating with traditional, even fundamentalist, American values.

Some may argue that to assimilate the Reagan administration, which has attempted to revive basic and highly ideological controversies about the contents of the federal agenda, to the category of rationalizing politics strains the term severely. Although the ideological fervor of this administration is admittedly rare by American standards, the practical politics of the Reagan years remain well within the rationalizing mode. First, even in the honeymoon following Reagan's commanding election victory of 1980, the reversal of breakthroughs was more a rhetorical means of stirring partisan and public opinion than a sustainable policy. Taking issue with Reagan's claim to have done "just about a 180-degree turn in the course of government," columnist George Will, a Reagan sympathizer, observed that neither Reagan's achievements nor his aspirations bear comparison with Franklin Roosevelt's accomplishments, which, by means of the managed economy and the welfare state, "altered, fundamentally and irrevocably, the relationship between the citizen and the central government." Whatever his private sentiments, Reagan has not called for the repeal of these federal responsibilities, Will noted. This is prudent politics, for if Reagan had appeared "bent on repealing the New Deal and dismantling the welfare state, Carter might have carried 44 states." Indeed, Will concluded that "Reagan won because he kept the election from being a referendum on conservative ideology."[31]

Second, in the Reagan administration, as in its immediate predecessors,

31. "About That Reagan Revolution," *Washington Post*, September 17, 1981.

the powerful dynamics of program growth remain largely intact. Two White House trial balloons on social security cuts were quickly popped amid cries that the president had unaccountably blundered. Modest, albeit highly controversial, reductions in benefits for consumers and reimbursements for providers in medicare and medicaid were enacted in 1981 and 1982, but the federal health budget is nonetheless expected roughly to double within five years.[32] When prospects faded for a competitive health care system, the promised "alternative to regulation," administration officials began talking of revenue caps and prospective reimbursement for hospitals. Funds for public service jobs were eliminated, but as unemployment rates rose the administration, House, and Senate soon developed new manpower measures; the main disputes were over the size of the authorization and whether the new program should be a block grant. In September 1982, with congressional elections impending and an unemployment rate of 10 percent threatening, Reagan called for rapid passage of the jobs measure, dubbing it a "hand up, not a handout." Reagan has proposed to return responsibility for welfare to the states, but as part of the swap has agreed to retain the food stamp program and to assume control of medicaid. Federal aid to cities has been cut, but the administration has offered a minor breakthrough of its own—urban enterprise zones.

Although the budget cuts signal "an important change in direction," they have not made a "deep penetration into the 1982 base of Federal spending,"[33] and total federal spending rose from 23 percent of the gross national product in fiscal 1981 to 24 percent in fiscal 1982.[34] Large increases in defense spending explain part of this figure, but economist Richard K. Vedder finds that of the $50.6 billion by which federal spending in the first nine months of fiscal 1982 exceeded expenditures in the same period of the previous year, $30.5 billion came from outside the Department of Defense. According to Vedder, it is a "myth" that the Reagan administration has achieved a dramatic reduction in federal spending. Indeed, "real government expenditures are increasing faster since President Reagan took office than they did under Jimmy Carter."[35]

Third, Congress has continued to prefer rationalizing to reversing. In the first budget battles with the new administration, the legislators bowed

32. Congressional Budget Office, *Baseline Budget Projections for Fiscal Years 1983–1987: A Report to the Senate and House Committees on the Budget—Part II*, February 1982, pp. 45–46.

33. Richard P. Nathan, quoted in *New York Times*, September 14, 1982.

34. John L. Palmer, quoted in ibid.

35. *Wall Street Journal*, August 30, 1982.

to sustained and skillful presidential pressure by enacting $27 billion in nondefense budget cuts; most of this came from discretionary programs mainly benefiting the poor and defended by weak constituencies. For example, Congress agreed to combine twenty-three health programs (the precise number depends on one's definition of "program") into four block grant packages with budgets reduced by about 25 percent; the programs—including such activities as rodent control, hypertension treatment, and maternal and child care—were obvious targets of political opportunity. On the other hand, the legislators emasculated the proposed social services block grant, and the proposal for a $4.4 billion consolidation into two education block grants emerged as a single $589 million measure, missing the large and popular title I program and others that aid handicapped children. Although some of the poor have suffered severely from the budget cuts, programs have generally been trimmed, not eliminated, and little new authorizing legislation would be needed to restore the status quo ante.

The strongest demonstration of the rationalizing significance of the Reagan administration is its most "radical" accomplishment—the deep individual and corporate tax cuts of 1981. By reducing government revenues, these cuts, as a practical matter, forced politicians to constrain or cut growth of the public sector on pain of higher deficits. (As a matter of theory it need not have been so: had the tax cuts triggered the explosive growth supply side economics promised, revenues might have sustained a stable or even growing governmental agenda despite them.) The cuts reflected the consensus among both parties that taxes had reached heights that were both politically intolerable and detrimental to investment and economic growth. This view, coupled with the widely accepted view that large federal budget deficits are also politically and economically insufferable, has compelled a convergence on constraint. The Republicans argue not for dismantling the welfare state but rather for trimming it back to appropriate levels of support for the truly needy. The Democrats argue not for a new round of breakthroughs but rather for an equitable application of budgetary discipline and a humane definition of need.

Fourth, it is possible that the vehement rhetoric of the Reagan years is the product of a highly unusual convergence of social resentments that are subsiding. By the end of the 1970s a wide range of concerns—inflation, taxing, and spending (especially on welfare); crime and the lack of punishment that accompanied it; the excesses of compensation [36] in the name of

36. Heclo, "Issue Networks," p. 98.

racial justice (especially busing and affirmative action hiring); challenges to social mores (changing sex roles and the abortion dispute); and loss of American prestige in Vietnam and Iran—had come together with peculiar force to fashion less a conservative ideology than a new conservative mood and sensibility. Translating general resentment into a practical agenda has been no easier for Reagan than for his predecessors, however, and more nearly normal politics appear to be reemerging. Reagan's accession to power has assuaged some resentments and put the burden of proof of wisdom and virtue on the conservatives. Fresh resentments with more liberal overtones are arising over the administration's policies on such matters as defense, racial fairness, and environmental protection. It is possible that the balance of ideological forces will be restored, inviting a return in rhetoric as well as in reality to the temperate rationalizing style.[37]

Presidency: Institutional Change

Rationalizing politics change presidential institutions and the balance of power among components of the executive branch, as well as presidential style. These institutional changes strongly favor centralization within the executive office and White House. First, the greater the growth of government, the greater the concern with the growth and composition of the governmental budget, and so the greater the influence of the Office of Management and Budget (OMB) in policy decisions.

Second, the greater the number of governmental programs, the larger the number of coordination problems that arise in making programs work,

37. For example, presidential aspirant Senator Gary Hart, Democrat of Colorado, takes a "deliberately nonideological" approach, contending that the traditional options—the Democrats' big-government programs and Reagan's cuts in taxes and domestic spending, while increasing defense budgets—are "bankrupt." His alternatives—such as a consumption tax and a new mix of military technology—are "sometimes criticized as a bloodless, technocratic type of politics" (*Wall Street Journal*, May 6, 1982). Senator Robert Dole, Republican of Kansas, also thought to harbor presidential aspirations, no longer plays the "acid-tongued villain," finding that the "role of the moderate suits him better" (*New York Times*, May 14, 1982). Aside from Reagan and (perhaps) Senator Edward M. Kennedy, all of the widely named potential presidential candidates for 1984—Senator Howard Baker, Republican of Tennessee; Vice-President George Bush; former Vice-President Walter Mondale; Senator John Glenn, Democrat of Ohio; Hart; and Dole—are ideological moderates.

In September 1982, as it became clear that the Republican Senate of the 97th Congress would not enact such New Right priorities as legalized school prayer and a ban on abortion, freshman Republican Slade Gorton of Washington explained that "the way the press read the elections of 1980 was wrong. . . . Most of us are economic conservatives, but there aren't more than four or five who could be characterized as members of the New Right" (*New York Times*, September 25, 1982).

implementing corrections, or designing new programs to fit the existing mix. The greater the concern with coordination across departmental and programmatic lines, the greater the executive's fascination with new coordinative techniques (program- or zero-based budgeting, for example) and new coordinative personnel, and so the stronger the tendency to confer new powers on actors more central than (and therefore supposedly "above") the partial and particularistic actors whose separated jurisdictions constitute the problem.

Third, centralized arrangements spurred by anxiety about budgetary control and program coordination are given an additional strong boost by presidential concern about control of the bureaucracy. The more government does, the more active and visible become the federal bureaucrats who specialize in and feel deep commitment to their particular program. The stronger the bureaucracy's imputed proprietary interest in programs, the more anxious is a new president about his ability to take control and make things work under his leadership. Therefore, a major consequence of the growth of the governmental agenda is the growth of generalists in the Executive Office of the President (EOP) and White House staff to manage it and make it work.

Recent presidents have entered office overtly contemptuous and inwardly fearful of civil servants administering the breakthroughs of the past.[38] The search for control usually begins with the department head; the president pledges his allegiance to strong secretaries and even to cabinet government. This allegiance seldom lasts long because, despite all the political science wisdom on the department head's side, the qualities that make a good department head—a national reputation; the ability to work well with civil servants, Congress, the public, and interest groups; and a strong character and sense of independent judgment—are precisely the opposite of the characteristics of a trusted presidential confidant. Over time, policymaking becomes the site of frequent skirmishes between department heads and EOP aides and, over time, the latter tend to win out. The cumulative effect is that policymaking becomes ever more centralized and generalist-dominated. Department heads, fearful that the bureaucracy will

38. See James L. Sundquist, "Jimmy Carter as Public Administrator: An Appraisal at Mid-Term," *Public Administration Review*, vol. 39 (January–February 1979), pp. 3–11, especially pp. 7–8. Sundquist observes of the Carter administration, "Its cadre of amateur governmental managers took office with the same (some say an even greater) admixture of contempt and hostility toward the federal 'bureaucrats' that previous administrations had displayed" (p. 8). See also Herbert Kaufman, *Red Tape: Its Origins, Uses, and Abuses* (Brookings Institution, 1977), p. 27.

drown uncongenial proposals, exclude it and reach out instead to academics, task forces, policy analysts, and others for the bright ideas and new directions they seek. White House and OMB aides, fearful that the department heads have been captured by the bureaus or have gone into business for themselves, pull policymaking still more firmly into their own ranks and those of their own trusted advisers. When the experts in the civil service are thought to feel primary loyalty to the very programs the new administration is attempting to rationalize, the temptation to concentrate policymaking in an ever more central and tightly knit circle of EOP and White House generalists is apparently irresistible. Although the Watergate affair led some to identify these centralizing tendencies with the idiosyncrasies of Nixon's persona and administration, it is more accurate to regard these tendencies as inherent in rationalizing politics. If so, filling the White House with good people with a good command of the arguments against a large and powerful EOP will have little or no effect.

Congress: Legislative Style

Congressmen suffer as much as if not more than presidents from the discomforts of rationalizing politics. Like presidents, legislators are expected to be continually "doing something," and they prefer to do something that affords ample opportunities for credit claiming, advertising, and position taking (in David Mayhew's terms).[39] These self-promoting activities are most easily derived from breakthroughs, especially those that confer tangible benefits on constituents. Rearranging existing programs and thereby upsetting settled expectations in order to trim a percentage point or two from the rate of growth of the federal budget or of inflation, to improve administrative efficiency and coordination, or to streamline social programs carry few claims to credit or opportunities for advertising and position taking and may even harm or antagonize important constituencies. In the Hill-Burton program for hospital construction, the Kennedy-Corman and Long-Ribicoff national health insurance bills, and the Pell grants to undergraduates, authors and breakthroughs are coupled in everyday speech. By contrast, few members of the public remember or care who were the key legislative sponsors and promoters of HMOs, PSROs, or revenue sharing. (The scarcity of such exceptions as the Kemp-Roth tax cut bill

39. David R. Mayhew, *Congress: The Electoral Connection* (Yale University Press, 1974), pp. 49–77.

would appear to confirm the rule.) Rationalizing politics becloud the electoral connection.

Understandably, Congress approaches rationalizing politics in ways that minimize pain or even make a virtue of a necessity. First, legislators, like presidents, attempt to use rationalizing policies as the occasion for a breakthrough when possible. For example, in order to win legislative approval, the block grant programs of the early 1970s not only loosened federal strings on aid to local governments (the Nixon administration's main concern), but, as noted earlier, also gave sizable aid to localities that had received little or none before.

Second, Congress usually avoids rationalizing measures that run afoul of well-organized, intensely interested constituencies. It has declined to substitute incentive-based antipollution measures for regulatory approaches, for example, not only because proponents of the former have failed to spell them out in convincing detail but also because it does not wish to offend environmentalists.

Third, Congress experiments with less stringent rationalizing approaches in hopes of heading off more painful ones. For instance, it authorized a demonstration program to see whether the incentive-based HMO approach could contain medical costs and thereby eliminate the need to resort to regulation.

Fourth, when there is no appealing alternative to regulation (which may have been demanded or supported by vocal constituencies but still imposes the political costs of nay-saying and constraint), Congress tries to ease the pain. One strategy is to delegate regulation to a large degree. In the environmental protection field, Congress declared a number of ambitious goals (breakthroughs) and then delegated to the states the planning needed to achieve them, subject to regulations to be promulgated by the Environmental Protection Agency. In this way it displaced—to the states, the bureaucracy, and also to the courts and the private sector—the costs of implementing its regulatory scheme. In the health field, Congress established new state and local regulatory bodies such as health systems agencies (HSAs) and PSROs, funded them, and entrusted the nay-saying and constraining to them. Another legislative strategy is to construct programs that, at least in theory, honor positive and progressive goals along with uninspiring cost containment objectives. Thus the PSRO program was supposed to monitor and improve the quality of medical care as well as economize. The health planning program was charged with both improving access to care and overcoming duplication and waste. In the health care field, unlike some of the classically regulated industries, provider interests generally oppose regulation, and Congress has been unwilling to adopt regulatory programs that cannot be sweetened in these ways. It therefore rejected the Carter administration's request for a federal ceiling on hospital revenue increases, a stark proposal that could neither be delegated nor made to wear a hopeful and forward-looking face.

In the legislature as at the White House, the restrained, technocratic character of rationalizing policies changes the tone and complexion of politics: put simply, being a congressman—or, better put, being a legislator—ceases to be much fun, however safe one's seat. Attempting to rearrange settled social and economic patterns in the interest of saving the government money, confusion, inconvenience, or embarrassment is far less pleasurable than fighting to fulfill the mission of twentieth-century liberalism or to rescue the nation from the erosion of ancient and cherished liberties by the intrusive federal government. "The desires, the repinings, the sorrows, and the joys of the present time lead to nothing visible or permanent, like the passions of old men, which terminate in impotence."[40]

The satisfactions of constituency service and waxing eloquent on broad policy issues remain, but the specific satisfactions of building subcommittee, committee, and whole-house coalitions on behalf of new, progressive, important breakthrough legislation with one's name on it recede, replaced only by the obligation to push along unpopular or undramatic legislation, the one redeeming feature of which is that it rescues the government from pitfalls of its own making. One might hypothesize, therefore, that the strains of rationalizing politics fall with greatest severity on Richard Fenno's influence-oriented congressmen, that is, those oriented mainly to developing and wielding political influence within their legislative chamber.[41] (The rewards of serving one's constituency and of making speeches on behalf of preferred policy positions with little or no chance of adoption presumably remain more or less intact.) It would be interesting to know whether such legislators are disproportionately represented in the recently swelling ranks of retirees, and what effects these strains may have on the quality of legislative leadership.

Congress: Institutional Change

Rationalizing politics also bring important institutional changes to the Congress. These changes aim at enabling Congress to keep pace with a

40. Alexis de Tocqueville, *Democracy in America*, vol. 1 (Knopf, 1945), p. 11.
41. Richard F. Fenno, *Congressmen in Committees* (Little, Brown, 1973), pp. 2–5.

bureaucracy whose activities steadily expand in scope and scale and with EOP generalists increasingly bent on taking control of that bureaucracy. The growth of agency activities alone would account for increased congressional staffing and activism. Traditional oversight tools are simply too intermittent and broad-gauged to be adequate for big government. Growing centralization within the EOP has also increased the legislators' incentives to search for new ways to restore legislative-executive balance.

One major institutional change is an increase in congressional staff, especially committee staff. The rationale is straightforward: a small, fixed number of generalist legislators cannot keep abreast of a steadily growing governmental agenda and an ever more active executive branch bureaucracy and thereby maintain the constitutional coequality of their branch of government unless they enlarge their own staff resources.[42]

Another important institutional innovation arising from Congress's need to cope with "big" government is the budget system created in 1974. The budget committees are pure rationalizers, their only function being to assume an overall point of view on the governmental budget and then debate, set, and argue in defense of constraints on the more specialized work of the legislative and appropriations committees. A Congressional Budget Office (CBO) was also created along with these committees to aid them in their work and to give Congress a sophisticated analytical capacity that would allow it to hold its own with the executive.[43]

Early critics of the new budget process were convinced that it could not work; after all, Congress had experimented with similar self-disciplinary measures after World War II and had quickly abandoned them all. The innovations of 1974 have worked better than expected, however, presumably because the "new" Congress confronting "big" government takes its rationalizing tasks seriously.

In other ways too, Congress has responded not only to the growth of the executive bureaucracy but also to that of the EOP generalists, the chief executive's main hope of gaining control over the civil service. In prerationalizing days, the much-discussed lines of administrative responsibility and accountability ran, at least in theory, from middle- and lower-level bureaucrats to division and bureau chiefs to the department head, a politically

42. On growth of staff, see James L. Sundquist, *The Decline and Resurgence of Congress* (Brookings Institution, 1981), pp. 402–14, especially the numbers on p. 408. See also Allen Schick, "The Staff of Independence: Why Congress Employs More But Legislates Less," prepared for the Miller Center, University of Virginia, October 1980.

43. On these committees, see Allen Schick, *Congress and Money* (Washington, D.C.: Urban Institute, 1980).

appointed managerial generalist who represented the department and its clients to the president and represented the president in turn to them. Legislation worked its way up through departmental ranks under the leadership of the department head; once drafted in this way, it was worked over and reviewed by White House coordinators (budget office) and staff, but the department's lead role in drafting and working for legislation was never in question. (To what extent this textbook image conformed to reality is far from clear.) This image of executive lines of authority in turn encouraged and presupposed an appropriate congressional response, namely, that the legislature should concentrate on the broad features of policy and administration, refraining from interfering in the small details of legislation (which might unduly bind the administrator's hands) and of administration (so as not to compromise the administrator's ability to assume responsibility for the behavior of the agency).

The growth of the EOP generalists has changed Congress's understanding of its own role in the fabled lines of administrative accountability and responsibility. The traditional arguments for restraint assumed that departments are run by political executives who are subject to Senate confirmation, who routinely testify before and bargain with Congress, and who stand accountable to Congress and to the public, as well as to the president, for their actions. Over time, however, it has become clear that department heads may be challenged, upstaged, or even reduced to figureheads by EOP personnel, especially White House aides and OMB officials who are (in most cases) not subject to Senate confirmation, who do not testify before or bargain with Congress, and who think of themselves as the president's personal aides, not as public figures expected to justify their words and deeds outside the confines of the White House.[44]

The enlarged executive bureaucracy and increased centralization of presidential power in the White House and EOP have called forth legislative innovations that violate the restraints required by the older doctrine of

44. Excerpts from two of this author's interviews with health policymakers in the Nixon years illustrate the point. A former OMB executive recalled that in the early 1970s "OMB was involved with HEW all along, *lots* of involvement. Remember that Nixon and Ehrlichman pretty much expected OMB and the Domestic Council to be on top of it, to live in the halls of HEW." A former House health subcommittee staffer remembered congressional attitudes after Nixon's reelection in 1972: "There was no real bargaining with the administration on the HMO bill [passed in 1973], and on the planning law of 1974 there was *no* discussion. Remember the circumstances. It was 1972, Nixon was reelected. The first thing he did was call in resignations. . . . Ehrlichman said the White House and the president are going to run the government and they set about impounding funds and all the rest. Relations just broke down then."

responsibility. In recent years Congress has made various efforts "to regain the power of the purse," "to recapture the war power," "to take command of foreign policy," and "to tighten control over administration" by means of new oversight techniques and the legislative veto.[45] These practices (to which enlarged staffs are indispensable) have evoked strong protests from administrators and from many political scientists. Even observers who sympathized with such congressional assertiveness in the Nixon years, when the executive and legislative branches were occupied by different political parties and when lines of administrative accountability were continually upset by various centralizing plots,[46] wondered why it should persist in the more restrained climate of the Carter administration. The answer may be not that legislative improvisations tailored to the Nixon years have for some reason been retained beyond their useful life, but instead that the requisites of rationalizing politics continue to sustain them. Congress is adapting its own modes of control to deal more realistically with changing patterns of executive control, which themselves respond to the great growth in the scope and scale of the governmental agenda in recent years. The new executive calls for new techniques of legislative action and oversight.

A final legislative consequence of rationalizing politics is to upset widely held doctrines of congressional roles and functions, notably by blurring the familiar distinction between Congress's legislative role and its oversight role. The growing complexity and detail of breakthrough legislation, along with the tendency for more and more interest groups to be affected by it and therefore in some measure aggrieved by it (see below), mean that legislation no sooner passes and administrative regulations are no sooner issued than cries go up from various quarters that the program is flawed and in need of change. Rationalizing legislation (proposed amendments to repair the flaws) thus becomes the occasion of oversight, and oversight activities become the occasion when supporters and opponents try to build or derail coalitions in favor of change (that is, mount a legislative struggle). The distinction between oversight and legislation as alternative congressional roles and functions, never entirely clear or convincing, is made less so by rationalizing politics.

The continual tinkering with legislation (rationalizing measures to repair breakthroughs, then additional measures to rationalize what has been rationalized, and so on) has four major consequences. First, it gives ratio-

45. These are the titles of chaps. 8–12 of Sundquist, *Decline and Resurgence of Congress.*

46. For a review of these "plots" see Richard P. Nathan, *The Plot That Failed: Nixon and the Administrative Presidency* (Wiley, 1975).

nalizing legislation the appearance of being an experiment or demonstration on its first time out, for it may take years and many returns to the legislative shop before it is got right. The coming and going may contribute to the impression that the government suffers from overload.[47] Second, this tinkering gives an unsettled and tentative aura to governmental activity that contrasts strongly with the positive moral certitudes that customarily accompany breakthrough legislation. Third, it leaves major committees less time for work on new breakthrough legislation (for which there is also less demand), an effort that often detracted from interest in oversight in the past.[48] Fourth, it enhances the policy role of legislative staff, whose specialty is a command of the technical terms and details that often bore or annoy congressmen.

In sum, Congress increasingly becomes in fact the oversight body it has long been said to be in theory, but this oversight, unlike that envisioned in the texts, centers increasingly on amendment and repair of detailed statutory provisions that originated in Congress itself, often over the objections of the executive. The resulting mix of oversight and activism as Congress retrenches on breakthroughs but extends its innovative role in bill drafting is both new and peculiar.

Bureaucracy

The cutting edge of governmental growth is the bureaucracy. The larger the scope and scale of the governmental agenda, the larger the number and types of activities performed by civil servants; the larger the number of citizens whose lives are affected in some fashion by bureaucrats; the more numerous and severe the frictions these contacts create; and the more insistently politicians take the offensive against bureaucratic waste, inefficiency, laziness, introversion, overspecialization, unresponsiveness, and other alleged bureaucratic pathologies. Growth of government, in short, increasingly sets the citizenry on the defensive against bureaucracy and bureaucracy on the defensive against its political controllers.

As more breakthroughs are entrusted to the administrative process for

47. "Policies feed on each other; the more there are, the more there have to be in order to cope with new circumstances, effects on other policies, and unexpected consequences. New legislative amendments and new administrative regulations become a growth industry as each makes work for the others." Wildavsky, "Policy as Its Own Cause," p. 82.

48. For example, John F. Bibby, "Committee Characteristics and Legislative Oversight of Administration," *Midwest Journal of Political Science*, vol. 19 (February 1966), pp. 78–98, especially pp. 95–96.

the smoothing of rough edges and timely and sensitive implementation, bureaucratic "bungling" becomes evident on an ever larger scale. Inevitably, bureaucracy disappoints—partly because of unresolved, unresolvable tensions in program design; partly because increasingly detailed laws reduce administrators' room for accommodation and improvisation; partly because private-sector and state and local actors prove recalcitrant or wily; partly because of unforeseen events and complications; partly because of inadequate agency energy and insight; but mostly because, as James Q. Wilson has argued, bureaucrats are continually asked to honor norms that conflict with one another.[49]

Whatever the real reasons for bureaucracy problems (which of course vary from program to program), aggrieved interests and politicians alike find it convenient to let administrators take the blame. When the Health Care Financing Administration fails to hold down medicare costs and does not put an end to cheating and fraud in medicaid; when the Food and Drug Administration follows its statutory mandate to ban chemicals that apparently cause cancer; when the Department of Housing and Urban Development (HUD) insists that communities receiving block grants provide for community participation; or when the Environmental Protection Agency sets allowable levels of emissions from polluting factories, the bureaucracy inevitably makes new enemies and antagonizes old ones in all sectors of society. The source of these frictions usually lies as much if not more in provisions or omissions of law (that is, in the political process) as in the administrative process per se, but in almost all cases the bureaucracy is an attractive object of blame.

This is the case for two reasons. First, by blaming the bureaucracy, interest groups and politicians may bargain with one another, communicating intentions subtly and without loss of face. The interest group spokesman who blames his constituents' ills directly on an important politician (the subcommittee chairman who authored the offensive law, for instance) risks a public quarrel and possible retaliation. By attributing his many woes to the bureaucracy, he makes his substantive points perfectly clear while allowing the politician to agree and promise legislative redress "to straighten the administrators out," without embarrassment. As the governmental agenda grows and frictions between government and groups multiply, this type of oblique bargaining at the administrators' expense increases.

49. James Q. Wilson, "The Bureaucracy Problem," *The Public Interest*, no. 6 (Winter 1967), pp. 3–9.

Second, the strategy is irresistibly attractive in the United States, where political culture is and has long been profoundly antibureaucratic. A Jacksonian-minded nation in love with the wisdom of the people and with the prospect of maximizing their self-rule has never taken kindly to being pushed around by appointed civil servants, and politicians know it.[50] The appeals of antibureaucratic rhetoric are recognized and exploited by Republicans and Democrats and by left and right alike; indeed, it is one of our major unifying political symbols. As bureaucracy and its misdeeds, real and imagined, grow along with government, it is not surprising that this rhetoric grows too. Virulent antibureaucratic outbreaks always follow breakthrough periods: examples include the reaction to New Deal "social planners" in the Roosevelt years, hysteria over the loyalty of State Department officials in the McCarthy years as the United States maintained its new international power in the Korean War, and Nixon's bureaucrat baiting during the 1968 presidential campaign in the wake of the Great Society. Jimmy Carter readily perceived the all-purpose character of the appeal and by means of promises to clean up "the mess" in Washington he exploited both specific disgust over Watergate and more general displeasure with the bureaucracy resulting from the policy accumulations of the Johnson-Nixon years. And Reagan's pledge to get government "off the people's back" is of course faithful to the genre.

These discontents usually lead rationalizing politics to make strenuous efforts to "debureaucratize" breakthrough programs. Five of the seven rationalizing modes listed earlier aim at finding alternatives to bureaucratic control (incentives), reducing or eliminating it (decentralization, disengagement, and deregulation), or improving its performance (reorganization). Moreover, even when obliged to resort to the other two modes, planning and regulation, policymakers may try to limit bureaucratic power. Thus, in the health field, the planning program relies primarily on local bodies representing providers, consumers, and major organizations, and the PSRO program uses peer review (that is, physician self-regulation).

Although there is too little experience with and too little research on the effectiveness of these antidotes to bureaucracy to allow a judgment, it would be surprising if they eliminated many frictions. For one thing, bureaucratization lies very much in the eye of the beholder: physician peer review, for example, may be far less bureaucratic than, say, government-

50. Sundquist, "Jimmy Carter as Public Administrator," p. 4.

imposed fee schedules, but to physicians unaccustomed to government-inspired review, it is bureaucratic enough to offend.

Second, the alternative to bureaucratic efforts at control may be incremental or wholesale abandonment of statutory goals and requirements. Efforts by HUD, for example, to ensure that localities receiving block grants obey controversial sections of the law have evoked fears of "recategorization."[51] As Kaufman remarks, even the best-intended and -designed governmental pronouncement "inevitably entails ambiguities." To align policies with intended purposes government must be "constantly clarifying categories," which of course means that "red tape tends to beget more red tape."[52]

Third, even efforts at nonbureaucratic rationalizing inescapably lock groups, new and old, in new conflicts with federal agencies. For instance, the incentive-based HMO program brought the Group Health Association of America, the HMO lobby, into continuing negotiations with the Department of Health, Education, and Welfare for the first time, and an important but elliptical provision of the HMO law—requiring employers to offer a federally qualified HMO as part of health benefit plans extended to employees—created new and bitter controversies between HEW and organized labor.

Fourth, breakthroughs inevitably increase the scope and scale of agency-group relations. If, for example, the federal government adopts a comprehensive energy policy, the already large bureaucratic presence in this policy area will expand enormously. In sum, no effective antidote to bureaucracy is at hand.

In one important respect, however, the war on bureaucracy has enjoyed some success. As noted above, presidential fears of an uncontrolled bureaucracy loyal above all to program maintenance and ready to drown innovative proposals have spawned numerous efforts to reassert generalist control.[53] Although these stratagems come and go, three apparently transcend the enthusiasm of particular administrations. First, as noted above, policymaking has been increasingly concentrated in the hands of EOP and

51. Richard P. Nathan and Paul R. Dommel, "Federal-Local Relations under Block Grants," *Political Science Quarterly*, vol. 93 (Fall 1978), pp. 421–42, especially pp. 426–27. On the costs of devolution, see Kaufman, *Red Tape*, pp. 71–77.

52. Kaufman, *Red Tape*, p. 86.

53. For the Nixon years, see Nathan, *The Plot That Failed*. On organizational issues from Franklin Roosevelt through Nixon, see Stephen Hess, *Organizing the Presidency* (Brookings Institution, 1976). On problems of generalists see Hugh Heclo, *A Government of Strangers* (Brookings Institution, 1977).

White House generalists. Second, these generalists have often snubbed the bureaucracy as a source of expertise, turning instead to policy analysts. They may, for example, call in academics and other supposed experts outside the government as consultants, advisers, "in and outers" in high positions, or members of task forces. Or they may enlarge EOP staff or the staffs of the secretaries and assistant secretaries of the departments with graduates of university public policy programs or other policy specialists with substantive expertise.[54] A third strategy, which has grown stronger in each recent administration, is to politicize ever deeper levels of the civil service.[55] The cumulative result is the expansion of generalists in high places and a steadily growing separation between these generalists and agency specialists. Enlarged congressional staffs, which give legislators readier access to data and analysis and facilitate bill drafting, have further depreciated the bureaucracy's expertise and have accelerated its exclusion from policymaking.

There are several troubling features of these trends. One is that the persistent bureaucratic scapegoating rests on a substantial measure of dishonesty: it encourages the citizenry to believe that its problems arise from administrative whim, not from hard choices and trade-offs made by elected officials, not to mention downright confusion among them. A second is that the scapegoating buys politicians short-term absolution at the price of what may be a longer-term evaporation of confidence in the political system as a whole. (If enough "outsiders" seek election on the pledge to "clean up the mess in Washington" or get it off the people's back, and move inside, only to reemerge two or three years later blaming their many failures on the mess in Washington or on the oppressive tenacity of government, people are likely to conclude in time that the whole system is perverse.)

Third, there are inherent limitations to what generalists, even highly intelligent generalists, can accomplish in policymaking without the judicious use of specialists. Generalists, be they EOP officials, academic policy analysts, or degree-carrying public policy experts trained to draw decision trees, are typically incapable of supplying from within their own ranks the detailed familiarity with fact, precedent, political history, operational detail, and local expectations and realities needed to construct plausible policy proposals.[56] Political generalists are usually patron-centered, that is,

54. Heclo, "Issue Networks," pp. 112–13.

55. Sundquist, "Jimmy Carter as Public Administrator," pp. 7–8.

56. For a case in point, see Lawrence D. Brown, *Politics and Health Care Organization: HMOs as Federal Policy* (Brookings Institution, 1983), especially chap. 9.

knowledgeable about and interested in the perceptions and stakes of their patron—the president, for example. Academic types are usually skilled at producing theoretical scenarios that depend on complex "if . . . then" relationships that seldom hold true in the real world. The two types fail to compensate for one another's weakness. As a result, the executive's capacity to distinguish between good ideas and good policy strategies diminishes over time.

Interest Groups

As the scope and scale of the governmental agenda grow, a larger number of interest groups become more deeply implicated in it, that is, more interdependent with government. This may be especially the case in the United States, which favors "indirect administration" of programs by "intermediary organizations" as a means of suppressing the growth of the federal bureaucracy.[57] Growing interdependence gives rise to efforts by both partners to rationalize problems that arise. These efforts take place, however, in political conditions that are themselves changed by the fact of government's growth.

Government's growth changes four main aspects of government-group relations—their scope and scale, their nature and contents, their normative basis, and government's own stakes and perceptions of them. First, as government grows, more parts of government interact with more groups over more matters on more occasions. New programs may awaken or redefine the political consciousness of existing groups. For example, enticed by the freer flow of federal funds under block grants and revenue sharing, some rural organizations, previously fearful of Washington intrusion, stepped up their lobbying for federal aid.[58] The growth of intergovernmental programs led groups of mayors, governors, counties, and other governmental entities to set aside at least some of their differences and join forces as an intergovernmental lobby seeking to influence the size and design of federal grants-in-aid.

A new government program may bring to new prominence previously marginal and obscure groups, such as the Group Health Association of America in the HMO case. A new program may crown the efforts and

57. Heclo, "Issue Networks," p. 92. Also, Frederick C. Mosher, "The Changing Responsibilities and Tactics of the Federal Government," *Public Administration Review*, vol. 40 (November-December 1980), pp. 541-48.

58. See Rochelle Stanfield, "Small Cities Are on the Prowl for Help from Washington," *National Journal*, October 7, 1978, pp. 1597-1601.

invigorate the zeal of new groups seeking to corner a piece of public policy as their preserve, as environmental legislation did for new environmental protection groups in the late 1960s and early 1970s. And of course new federal intervention gives groups long accustomed to dealing routinely with the federal government—business firms, their trade associations, and umbrella groups like the Chamber of Commerce, for example—new items to contend over, such as the rising costs of antipollution and worker safety regulations.

Indeed, political energies that would previously have been channeled into public expenditure breakthroughs may increasingly be channeled into programs obliging the private sector to bear the costs of new benefits. Four recent cases in point are the Employee Retirement Income Security Act pension law, the affirmative action hiring requirements, the extension of the mandatory retirement age to seventy, and the newly legislated rights for the handicapped. These programs add relatively little to the federal budget, but disrupt private practices on a large scale. For activists facing a clogged and stagnant federal agenda, this breakthrough displacement by and from the federal government onto the private sector and state and local governments was a highly inviting political strategy. Since the mid-1960s it has been pursued vigorously and variously by means of statute, regulation, and litigation, with considerable success. Especially tempting have been the so-called crosscutting requirements, which oblige all recipients of federal aid to do (or refrain from doing) certain tasks at their own expense as a condition of receiving federal aid. Before 1964, the federal government imposed only eight such requirements, but between 1964 and 1980, the number rose to fifty-nine, thirty-six of which reflected "social or economic policy decisions." [59] The political costs of this success have been very high, however: the strategy has contributed greatly to private and subnational resentment of federal overregulation and to the impression that the federal government was on society's back.

New government programs and activities may also encourage the formation of new groups by sharpening issue consciousness surrounding government's doings. In the 1960s, largely as a result of heightened public consciousness produced by a breakthrough (the Supreme Court's 1954 decision that segregated schools are unconstitutional, which increased pressure for more breakthroughs, namely, civil rights legislation) and the

59. Anne H. Hastings, *The Strategies of Government Intervention: An Analysis of Federal Education and Health Care Policy* (Ph.D. dissertation, University of Virginia, 1982), p. 106.

misfortunes of American intervention in Southeast Asia, many new organizations formed rapidly. The civil rights movement began by revitalizing traditional organizations like the National Association for the Advancement of Colored People and the Congress of Racial Equality and then gave rise to new ones like the Student Nonviolent Coordinating Committee. The federal War on Poverty, much of it directed against the problems of central city blacks and encouraging their participation, led to more new groups—community development corporations, neighborhood health centers, and before long, national associations of corporations and centers. The intellectual and social energy released by the drive for equal rights for blacks then gave rise, by way of osmosis and highly contagious analogical thinking, to a broader concern for the rights of other "oppressed minorities" and thus begat organizations working for the equal rights of homosexuals, Hispanics, Indians, women, the handicapped, the elderly, the unborn, and others. Some of these groups eschewed politics in favor of a celebration of their newly raised group consciousness and life-styles. Most, however, adopted a political agenda and pursued it aggressively.

The larger the number of grant-in-aid and transfer programs, each with its own conditions and rules, adopted by the central government on behalf of minority or disadvantaged groups, the more government impinged on the budgets, politics, and administrative life of state and local officials. This development in turn encouraged *them* to organize and to build up their own staffs of policy specialists to defend their interests and explain their problems in Washington.[60] "To a very great extent," writes Samuel Beer in a study of the politics of general revenue sharing, "the incentive and pressure to organize . . . came from government intervention and the concerns and opportunities it presents."[61]

While the civil rights groups organized on behalf of the rights of minorities, the antiwar movement worked to build opposition to American foreign policy among the general public. These efforts produced a spreading interest in an assortment of "general publics" and "public goods" supposedly in need of the protection that organized political action brings.[62] (These groups also gave a home to reform-minded individuals who could no longer feel at home in the equal rights groups as the growth of black power and other separatist strands drove outsiders out.) Organizational results in-

60. Heclo, "Issue Networks," p. 100.

61. Beer, "The Adoption of General Revenue Sharing," p. 164.

62. For a wide-ranging discussion of these groups, see Jeffrey Berry, *Lobbying for the People* (Princeton University Press, 1977).

cluded the environmental and consumer protection movements, freewheeling reform efforts such as those associated with Ralph Nader and Common Cause, and the antinuclear movement. These groups were for the most part explicitly and zealously political, pressing the search for new breakthroughs and diligently superintending them once attained. By the early 1970s, the universe of political organizations was handsomely populated by groups widely discounted before as unorganizable for sociological reasons (the disadvantaged were thought to be too anomic to organize extensively)[63] and for economic reasons (general publics were said to be beset by collective goods and free rider problems). In all of these ways, accumulating governmental intervention has led to increases in the staff, organizational consciousness, Washington presence, and political activism of large formal organizations with a stake in what government does.[64]

Second, growth of government changes the nature (as distinct from the scope and scale) of group-government dealings. Facing faits accomplis (however they may have come about), groups that may earlier have fought to produce or block breakthroughs now enter into a bargaining relationship with government over the details of policy. Before the enactment of medicare, the federal government did not really bargain with the American Medical Association (AMA); the group's opposition to a major federal role in health insurance was nonnegotiable. Government did not then bargain with the HMO industry either; it had no reason to do so.

In the aftermath of medicare, it bargains with both groups. One reason for the change is that it is now in the groups' interest to bargain: physicians, recognizing that medicare is here to stay and that the federal government is increasingly concerned about its costs, work to keep federal cost containment proposals within acceptable limits. The HMO industry, observing that the federal government appears determined to launch HMOs that meet carefully defined criteria, works to ensure that the legislated criteria are acceptable to its members. Another reason for bargaining is that it is in government's interest. The medicare program runs much more smoothly if physicians accept medicare recipients, refrain from propagandizing against

63. In retrospect, the conventional wisdom appears to be correct. The antipoverty groups seldom lasted long, rarely enrolled many members, and were heavily dependent on the organizational efforts of the upwardly mobile.

64. This population soon grew even larger as new groups underwent organizational fission. Disputes about the relative emphasis to be given to the cultural celebration of group life-style versus the quest for political gain in the equal rights groups sometimes generated two, three, or more groups from one. The trend was especially evident in the women's rights, gay rights, and consumer protection fields.

the program, and comply voluntarily with its regulations. If the HMO industry brands the HMO program as unworkable, this decreases the enthusiasm of sponsors and entrepreneurs for starting new plans with its assistance.

Government, in short, seeks means of mobilizing consent.[65] As government interacts with more groups over more details, the costs of conflict—in time, aggravation, paperwork, uncertainty, and wasted effort—increase. This increases the value of reducing conflict by mobilizing the consent of the major organizations that stand between government and constituencies and economic sectors (doctors or HMO sponsors, for example) and therefore stand between government intention and program outcome.

Third, growth of government introduces subtle but important changes in the normative bases of government-group interaction. The new single-issue interest groups are often said to practice "ideological" politics at odds with traditional American pragmatism. Although it is true that American politics have never been highly ideological by European standards and are now even less so than they were in the past,[66] the ideology-pragmatism dichotomy misses the central point. Both contemporary American politics and those of the single-issue groups are better described as "principled." Principled politics are an effort to advance a value judgment by means of public policy. Ideological politics are the effort to advance an *integrated system* of value judgments by means of policy. Ideological politics are at once divisive—generating conflict between large social blocs with antagonistic, comprehensive visions of the proper relations among state, economy, and society—and integrative—giving sizable groups stable, consistent positions across a range of policy issues. Principled politics are at once disaggregative—permitting issues to be trotted out and agitated individually in detachment from other issues—and disintegrative—fragmenting political positions among legions of special-purpose organizations, each specialized in the protection and advancement of its cherished principles.

Ideological politics are sustained by breakthrough struggles—for exam-

65. The term is taken from Samuel H. Beer. See his "The British Legislature and the Problem of Mobilizing Consent," in Elke Frank, ed., *Lawmakers in a Changing World* (Prentice-Hall, 1966), pp. 30–48.

66. As Anthony King observes, "It is now all but impossible to infer a person's views on one range of subjects from his or her views on another range." "The American Polity in the Late 1970s: Building Coalitions in the Sand," in King, *New American Political System*, p. 372. On reasons why the end of ideology "seems more applicable to the political discourse of the 1970s than it was to the period in which it was coined, the 1950s," see Greenstein, "Change and Continuity in the Modern Presidency," pp. 70–71.

ple, over whether the federal government should create a program of medical assistance for the poor or regulate industrial pollution of the air and water. But once such a program is adopted, and debate turns to the wisdom of adjusting its details, ideology tends to give way to disputes about principle—should medicaid funds be used to pay for abortions? Are copayments for medical services an equitable means of reducing costs? Are clean air and water commodities fit for buying and selling?—and about empirical, analytic issues—will the poor simply resort to unsafe means of abortion if they are denied public funds? Do copayments raise costs by discouraging consumers from seeking care until they get sick? Can one design a scheme of pollution taxes and rights that is neither too stringent nor an invitation to continued pollution as costs are passed along to consumers? In short, growth of government gives more groups more frequent occasions to attack or defend ever longer lists of principles that government programs have newly acknowledged, made implicit, or given reconsideration. If class and sectoral conflict is the mode of ideological politics, single-issue groups brandishing technocratic policy analyses in defense of cherished principles is that of rationalizing politics, a mode that diffuses conflict and increases fragmentation.

Another important normative consequence of growing government is a redefinition of the meaning of equity or fairness to groups. In debates over breakthroughs, the central question has been equity (or equality) for disadvantaged groups. As these programs multiply, however, concern grows for those asked to finance and carry them out. In the United States, which extensively delegates central governmental commitments to state and local governments, complaints about federal strings or matching financial requirements accompany each new effort, as the intergovernmental lobby emphasizes. And because the United States also relies heavily on the private sector to deliver the human services to which the poor are entitled, problems arise for physicians, housing developers, and others about remuneration levels or the definition of acceptable services. These providers too depend on their Washington representatives to dramatize the unfairness of their plight and the case for redress. Finally, because the United States lacks a political culture with a deeply rooted normative endorsement of the welfare state, appeals about the injustice of middle-class taxpayers footing the bill for new governmental programs strike an ever more responsive chord, as the successful politics of California's Proposition 13 and of Reagan's tax-cut campaign pledges demonstrate.

In sum, as government grows, the rhetoric of equity and equality for the poor gives way to the technical terminology of efficiency and to a new concern about equity for providers. Rationalizing politics oblige government to mediate between the organized guardians of beneficiaries and providers, both newly enlivened by the stimulus of government's own efforts and both well staffed and prepared to debate the equity of program details.

Fourth, growth of government brings a change in the government's own approach to groups. For a variety of reasons, in postbreakthrough policy arenas policymakers tend to be unwilling simply to umpire struggles among social groups and to register periodically in policy the balance of social or group power. When the question is not what government should be doing but rather the effects of what government is already doing, government is likely to come to the bargaining table armed with an agenda of its own. If uncontrollable medicare or social services spending increasingly dominates the federal health or social services budget, policymakers have a direct interest in seeking means of control. In the search the AMA (for example) will be consulted, perhaps bargained with; but it will be at most a pressure group, not the veto group of premedicare days. Political leaders may even find the courage to challenge the "iron triangles" that dominate many policy arenas in more placid circumstances. No longer will any outcome acceptable to the range of interested groups be automatically acceptable to government. Rationalizing politics are a government-led search for solutions to government's problems.

The net result of these developments seems paradoxical: government and groups become at once more interdependent (bargaining over more points of concern to more groups and parts of government) and more detached (government develops interests and commitments of its own). As yet, there seems to be no adequate vocabulary or model to capture this odd trend. Looking at the former condition, one may conclude that government is more and more run by special-interest groups, that interest group liberalism has run rampant. Looking at the latter condition, however, one might conclude that interest group liberalism is but half the story, and that the growth of public-sector, rationalizing politics and endogenous governmental commitments and initiatives has on the whole reduced the power of interest groups.

When breakthrough programs go awry, government and groups may well differ on the proper means of correction. Rationalizing politics may therefore be the scene of protracted and repeated government-group bargaining that produces outcomes that are unsatisfying, or only temporarily satisfying, to one side or both. Rationalizing politics thus take on a self-sustaining quality, their work never done.

As growth and the need to cope with its consequences put government in recurrent contact with more groups, occasions for frustration and irritation over legislative and administrative requirements grow more numerous. Three consequences follow. First, both the private sector and the legion of public interest groups who fancy themselves protectors of public programs send up a rising chorus of complaint about the perversity and irrationality of government, most especially the federal bureaucracy. As a rule, these groups register different complaints: the private sector argues that government has gone too far, the public interest groups that it has not gone far enough. In short, government appears to command legitimacy and the confidence of major group elites in inverse proportion to the scope and scale of its activities: the more it does, the less elite support it garners and retains.

Second, these groups and their supporters in government generate a steady stream of legislative proposals to eliminate major sources of friction. (Referring to a bill to subject Federal Trade Commission regulations to a legislative veto, a leading congressional proponent observed that "[Federal Trade Commission Chairman] Mike Pertschuk is doing the best job of promoting my bill. . . . Every time he issues another rule, we pick up another trade association that didn't know it applied to them.")[67] The result is the convergence, described above, of legislative and oversight roles in Congress and a growing legislative workload devoted to refining the details of breakthroughs or of previous rationalizing policies.

A third consequence resulting from the application of more detailed laws and regulations to more of the affairs of more groups is a growing demand that the courts resolve conflicts between groups and government over the proper interpretation of complex statutory texts and intentions. A litigious society can only become more so as government grows.[68]

Political Parties

Many observers react to the developments described above with dismay, even with alarm. In a political system with a high degree of formal decen-

67. Quoted in Burt Schorr, "Slowing Down the FTC," *Wall Street Journal*, July 30, 1979.

68. See Donald L. Horowitz, *The Courts and Social Policy* (Brookings Institution, 1977); R. Shep Melnick, *Regulation and the Courts: The Case of the Clean Air Act* (Brookings Institution, forthcoming); and Rand E. Rosenblatt, "Health Care Reform and Administrative Law: A Structural Approach," *The Yale Law Journal*, vol. 88 (December 1978), pp. 243–336.

tralization, the growth of interest groups and their demands, the expansion of bureaucratic roles and powers, the legislature's determination to improvise means of keeping pace with the executive, and the growing disposition of legislature and executive alike to "manage the government," not "lead the nation," may simultaneously aggravate both overload and fragmentation to the point of crisis. To many critics, the best answer—indeed, the only plausible answer—lies in an informal centralizing mechanism that will promote coordination among institutions, support concerted action by political leaders, and represent the masses outside the interest group system in order to contain demands, overcome fragmentation, and ensure truly democratic representation. That informal centralizing mechanism is, of course, the political party.

Few who advocate a larger party role in U.S. politics find much solace in present trends. Indeed, because many of the worrisome developments noted above appear to be linked to the decline of U.S. parties, some journalists and political scientists have argued with renewed urgency the importance of reversing this decline and strengthening the party system, preferably by means of responsible parties that give the electorate a clear, distinct, and principled choice among stands on issues of the day.

An equally, perhaps more, logical inference from the correlation between deplored facets of the new politics and party decline is that parties, far from being an antidote to these problems, are doomed to suffer along with other institutions in the general play of cause and effect. This at any rate is the argument that will be briefly developed here.

Government growth and the rise of rationalizing politics contribute to a host of social and political developments—including the spread of presidential primaries, changes in party rules and personnel, the growing influence of the media, and new methods of financing campaigns—that erode the cohesion of political parties, the allegiance they command among the electorate, and their independent influence on policymaking. Policy of course is not the only or perhaps even the main force behind the decomposition and collapse that most observers find in the present U.S. party system. Unfortunately, students of U.S. parties have relied heavily on quantitative analyses that treat party identification as a correlate of the votes or attitudes of various population groups categorized by age, sex, income, education, and the like. Too few studies treat parties primarily as organizations, rather than as entities whose qualities are to be inferred from numerical associations between attributes of groups and votes and attitudes. Therefore one can do little more than speculate about the corrosive forces at work.

No attempt is made here at a comprehensive account of the reasons for party decline. Given the paucity of careful organizational analyses of present party trends, three hypotheses relevant to the limited purposes pursued here may be useful. One is that political parties should be viewed as one of a substantial and growing number of voluntary associations in an organizational marketplace whose elements must compete for the allegiance, efforts, and resources of actual and would-be contributors.[69] A second hypothesis is that the relative attractiveness of parties to contributors over time will depend on the opportunity cost of contributing to them. This in turn depends on the appeals of parties relative to those of the organizational competition. A third hypothesis is that party decline may be explained in part by the coincidence of two trends: government growth and the rise of rationalizing politics have depreciated the value of party appeals even as larger numbers of attractive organizational alternatives have entered the marketplace. The result is a substantially increased opportunity cost of party allegiance.

As James Q. Wilson has argued, political parties, like other voluntary associations, must sustain themselves by maintaining an incentive system that offers contributors an attractive combination of material, solidaristic, and purposive rewards. Material-based parties emphasize tangible rewards for loyalists, usually money or jobs. These rewards generally involve corruption and patronage. Solidaristic parties emphasize fellow feeling among friendly and like-minded subgroups. Purposive parties attract members to their ideologies or goals. No real-world party is a pure type of one incentive system alone, of course; the essence of a party's constituency and character lies in the mix.

In the United States, government growth and the consequent rationalizing politics seem to be eroding all three types of inducement to party activity. Both the supply of and the demand for party-based material inducements have declined. The growth of entitlement programs financed by the central government is part of a long-term, steady trend in which government confers welfare benefits by right, not at the discretion of party functionaries. Indeed, a major consideration in most of the federal welfare breakthroughs has been to overcome and avoid the abuses of political and administrative discretion found in earlier efforts at the state and local

69. See Wilson, *Political Organizations*, pp. 95–118, on which the following account of party incentive systems draws heavily.

levels. The growth of federal welfare programs in the New Deal is one widely offered explanation of the decline of central-city political machines.[70] These programs, hemmed in by statutory and administrative eligibility criteria that reduce official discretion, are also increasingly administered by nonpartisan officials, a consequence of decades of reform and of declining local taste and tolerance for corruption. In sum, as entitlements grow, the electorate depends more on government, but less on party.

The impact of government growth on solidaristic allegiances to parties is more difficult to judge because parties so sustained have not received the attention given to the machine and because most of the few studies that address this mode of attachment are dated.[71] Several factors, few having much to do with growth of government, have devalued the local party clubhouse as a source of camaraderie and fun: racial transitions in older inner-city neighborhoods, class and geographic mobility (leading to suburbanization and an attenuation of ethnic consciousness) among second- or third-generation ethnics, television's tendency to replace the political headquarters as a source of entertainment, and—perhaps most important and more closely linked to governmental growth—the rise of organizational alternatives to the political party for like-minded activists (or inactivists) who enjoy sharing one another's company.

Growth of government weakens purposive attachments to party as surely as it weakens material ones. Major issue areas that sustain breakthroughs come to be preoccupied with unexpected, puzzling, and complex difficulties. Familiar party and ideological positions fail to yield plausible policy answers in individual issue areas, and, equally important, fail to offer solutions that make sense across issue areas and thereby add up to a coherent, persuasive ideology or public philosophy.

When policymakers are obliged to grapple with such problems as medical cost inflation, rigidities in the categorical grant-in-aid system, or the proper degree of government control over competition in transportation and related industries, answers may seem to lie in odd and previously unattractive mixes of incentives, deregulation, regulation, planning, reorganization, and even disengagement. Prominent political figures may embrace a seemingly conservative option in one area (Senator Kennedy, for example, working for airline deregulation), and a liberal stance in others (Kennedy

70. William Foote Whyte, *Street Corner Society* (University of Chicago Press, 1943), pp. 196–98; and Edward C. Banfield and James Q. Wilson, *City Politics* (Harvard University Press, 1963), p. 121.

71. See the discussion and references in Wilson, *Political Organizations*, pp. 110–15.

working for a hospital cost containment regulatory scheme), while other areas (HMOs, for example) cannot be classified in traditional categories at all.

Most of these strategies, as noted above, are government's answers to government's problems; they usually neither emanate from nor reverberate in local constituencies. In the odd case where constituency stakes in a rationalizing program are deeply felt—the possibility that the hospital cost ceiling would force closings or cutbacks at local hospitals, for example—citizens may write to their congressmen or may support the political efforts of directly affected interests such as hospital leadership or the local medical society. The local party (such as it is) will have little or no role in agitating the issue.

The complexity of the issues and the absence of ideologically consistent solutions across areas encourage a loss (or, perhaps better, fragmentation) of purpose, the dominance of technique, a weakening of party zeal, and a blurring of ideological disagreements. One fundamental reason is that agenda convergence plays havoc with party norms and positions. Democrats (no longer pushing eagerly for the latest in a series of welfare state triumphs) and Republicans (fighting to slow the growth of programs they cannot and usually would not repeal) have converged reluctantly on arcane quests for managerial and budgetary repairs to the handiwork of the political giants of the past. The organizational identities of one or both parties may thus lose focus.[72] That zeal and disagreements remain strong in prebreakthrough areas, or areas approaching the breakthrough stage, merely aggravates the situation, for the coexistence of the breakthrough and rationalizing modes makes the synthesis of a general ideological or partisan stance that much more difficult. That no ideological position today yields a comprehensive set of highly persuasive answers to policy questions in any major issue area, let alone the entire range, is bound to be unsettling to those who value cognitive consistency, the having of convictions and the courage of them, or the simple self-satisfaction of knowing exactly where one stands on major issues of the day.

Those acquainted with the comparatively restrained and sweetly reasonable (although perplexing and principled) debates over the application of

72. Both the Democrats and Republicans suffered a protracted struggle over ideological focus between at least 1968 and 1980. The struggle continues more sharply then ever among the Democrats, as such new coinages as "boll weevils" and "neoliberals" contend with traditional liberals, and although the Republicans came abruptly into focus in 1980 with the election of Ronald Reagan, it will be surprising if their harmonious homogeneity lasts long.

incentives, decentralization, deregulation, regulation, planning, reorganization, and even disengagement to policy problems today may have trouble recalling that in the heat of breakthrough struggles political parties have sometimes resembled (as Henry Adams wrote of early Massachusetts politics) "the systematic organization of hatreds."[73] Such passion rarely carries over to debates about how problems arising from breakthroughs should be rationalized. Agenda convergence progressively drains away much of the partisan principle from the program divergence that remains. Or to put the point another way, in rationalizing politics, policy realignment is ever less dependent on partisan realignment.[74]

The weakening of the parties' organizational incentive systems is but part of the explanation of their decline. Of equal or greater importance is the rapid entry into the organizational marketplace of the many new and attractive alternatives to political party activity, mentioned above. These raise the opportunity cost of party activity. Increasingly, our "middle-classified,"[75] indeed upper-middle-classified, society is beyond the reach of the material stakes of politics and disdainful of old-fashioned clubhouse companionship; it seeks and finds a new synthesis of solidaristic and purposive political rewards in new special-purpose organizations that embody its principled political style. It is perfectly rational and natural that the middle and upper-middle political classes, too sophisticated to be more than intermittently ideological, but too concerned to be apolitical, should prefer the special-purpose organization to the catchall political party as a vehicle of political participation. Those led to participate by issue consciousness, that is, by a desire to contribute to the realization of specific political goals—an end to the war, an end to the slaughter of seals, passage of the equal rights amendment, or preservation of the environment—have much more to gain by joining or contributing to special-purpose organizations, devoted to and staffed for single-minded, full-time pursuit of declared principles. In contrast, a general-purpose American party (which one cannot really "join," a terminological difference of great practical significance) must of necessity

73. *The Education of Henry Adams* (Houghton Mifflin, 1961), p. 7.

74. Writing in 1965 with evidence from surveys taken in the 1950s and early 1960s, Robert E. Lane found a "declining sense of crisis, declining perception of threatened policies that might endanger the country, and declining belief that personal or group welfare is involved in an electoral decision," in short, a growing "indifference" to the outcomes of elections. Partisanship, he found, remained strong but had "lost some of its 'bite' and acrimony" ("Politics of Consensus," p. 884). Such attitudes, one might surmise, would make policy change less dependent on partisan realignments than had been the case before.

75. The term is John Dollard's, in Banfield, *The Unheavenly City Revisited*, p. 52.

blur and aggregate multigroup interests and purposes into a mèlange minimally acceptable to all and fully acceptable to none. In the words of Republican pollster Robert Teeter, "In many ways, the special interest groups, whether from the left or the right, have taken over and become the kind of ad hoc political parties of our time, because they're the ones who have bound people of like mind together to bring about change."[76]

The new equal rights and general-interest organizations of the 1960s and 1970s were quick to recognize that the struggle for breakthroughs for their particular constituencies and causes, and the constant, strident superintending of them, were crucial to their maintenance and growth. Most of them therefore threw themselves with great energy into creating new legislation and monitoring the administration of existing laws. Although the groups have been anything but shy about pressuring the system, most of them have maintained a fastidious principled detachment from sustained partisan identifications, alliances, and activities.

As has often been recognized, these organizations offer a new and expansive set of alternatives to party activity for the political stratum, and therefore may be themselves an important cause of party decline. (They are also in some degree a response to it.) The new groups are not entirely divorced from party activity, of course, but they tend to be highly selective, independent, and fickle, infuriating politicians by refusing to line up with parties on the limited issues of concern to them; by threatening to withhold support, move to the opposition, or even found their own political party unless their demands are met; by being rigid and slow to bargain and compromise; and by occasionally targeting enemies—in "dirty dozen" lists, for example—to be defeated on election day.

The decline of party and the proliferation of special-purpose organizations are bringing about changes in the nature of candidate appeals and campaigning. The successful candidate of present and future is one who not only avoids offending the great middle range of the bell-shaped curve but also astutely picks his or her way across the minefields of single-issue organizations, deftly maximizing "correct" position fragments. Even as party

76. Quoted in *New York Times*, November 9, 1980. As several observers have remarked, the growing power of the special-interest group at the expense of parties appears to be a long-term trend, not a sudden development. For instance, Theodore J. Lowi notes that "nationally organized interest groups" offered "political alternatives to the parties in policy formulation" from the late nineteenth century, and even earlier at the state level. By 1900 "parties in Congress went into a decline from which they have never fully recovered" ("Four Systems of Policy, Politics, and Choice," *Public Administration Review*, vol. 32 [July–August 1972], pp. 301–02). See also Wilson, *American Government*, p. 609.

nostalgia buffs argue the need to make U.S. parties more responsible, the new conditions carry candidates to ever greater heights of irresponsibility and obfuscation. Traditional, partisan, "role-of-government" issues count for steadily less in a nation committed to a managed economy, international leadership, and a welfare state. The newer concerns that may make or break a winning electoral coalition—inflation, civil rights, crime, feminism, abortion, nuclear power, the environment, consumer protection, and the cost of energy and medical care—for the most part lack clear partisan dimensions, that is, they do not tend systematically, distinctly, and enduringly to divide Democrats from Republicans, or even liberals from conservatives.

The successful candidate of today is likely to seem amorphous and disturbing to those who value partisan principle and issue consistency. Moreover, if such a candidate wins office and finds himself obliged to make trade-offs as he tries to make policy, his coalition of finicky organizations may feel betrayed, may denounce him as a "politician as usual," and may then come apart, as the coalition's components flirt with or move to a challenger whose position on their paramount issue is more nearly pure. (Ronald Reagan, for instance, is by the standards of most American presidents a model of focused consistency, but after little more than a year in office he found himself defending the largest peacetime federal budget deficit in history, under attack for showing insufficient mettle in punishing Communist abuses in Poland and Latin America, and a disappointment to moral majoritarians who had hoped that his presidency would carry the day for their arguments on various social issues.)

It may be objected that none of this is new. After all, past politicians were evasive and inconsistent, and electoral coalitions have been known to disintegrate. Although the differences described here are admittedly ones of degree, they are no less real for that. In the past, a candidate could, by uttering the right partisan buzzwords in the right places, buy tolerance for ambiguity on other issues before other audiences. Today, the old partisan buzzwords do not have the desired effect, no new ones have replaced them ("trust," "love," "balanced budget," and "magic of the marketplace" do not qualify) and the campaigner's skill lies not only in knowing how to appear to take positions without committing oneself but also in knowing how to honor a wide range of specialized groups with the right position without exposing the accumulating inconsistencies and impracticalities of items on the list. In the past, major elements of supportive electoral coalitions were usually willing to watch and wait, to compromise and aggregate, and if not to forget some trespasses at least to forgive in anticipation of coming elections. Today groups are more likely to seek rapid and literal fulfillment of the promises they thought they heard and, if disappointed, feel little shame in denouncing or ignoring their erstwhile ally, in withdrawing support, or even in threatening alliances with right-thinking public figures of quite different ideological or partisan persuasions.

The Carter administration, which this description may bring to mind, will probably prove to be not a stylistic aberration born of the peculiarities of presidential politics of the mid-1970s, but instead a harbinger of the political future. The less attractive features of the style—the sudden national love-in with a newcomer whose principles are vague but whose positions are all "correct," the rapid sense of national drift and group betrayal as positions are (or are not) transformed into proposals and programs, the consequent erosion of presidential popularity by midterm or sooner, the rising infatuation with a new figure with a magic formula guaranteed to set things right, and, as a result of all this, the nation's declining ability to feel governed—will not be easily eliminated.

It would be reckless to assert that special-purpose groups have achieved a stranglehold on the electoral and policy processes. As the 1980 presidential election made plain, broad and general issues of transcendent interest to the electorate—inflation, American international prestige and military power, the decline of morality, for example—may sweep over specific group agendas and in the process sweep one administration out and another in. If these groups are less than omnipotent in the electoral process, however, they are extremely influential in the nominating process, especially in the primaries and in fund raising; they play a major role in withholding or conferring legitimacy as officeholders try to govern; and they may indeed wield great electoral clout at times when broad, crosscutting issues are in short supply or of low intensity.

If the framework used here is valid, it is useless to bewail the decline of parties and still more useless to argue that somehow strong parties in a responsible party system should be erected on the parties' decrepit foundations. These arguments, long-debated and long-debunked, are even less tenable today than ever. First, as has been pointed out repeatedly, the preconditions of responsible parties are consistent neither with U.S. political structures (which, among other complications, separate congressional from presidential nominating processes), nor with U.S. social structures (which benefit from blurring, not sharpening, differences among races, classes, regions, and nationalities).[77]

Second, although the theoretical case for complementing decentralized formal structures with informal centralizing mechanisms is impeccable, practice is another matter. That a strong party organization helped Richard Daley to govern Chicago[78] does not mean that something similar can be devised to help a Carter or Reagan to govern the United States. As Arthur Schlesinger, Jr., recently pointed out, even Franklin Roosevelt "in the era of so-called rubberstamp Congresses, had to fight for every New Deal measure after the Hundred Days and, with all his craft and popularity, was not uncommonly defeated on cherished initiatives."[79]

Finally, despite many windy declamations about the mass representational functions of parties, little empirical evidence has been gathered on the subject in the United States. (Although there is a sizable literature on urban political machines, for example, it is all but impossible once one gets beyond anecdotal evidence about hods of coal and ethnic ticket balancing to estimate the extent to which these organizations benefited the working classes.) Much of the talk about mass representational functions of parties in the United States seems to rest on imaginative transpositions to these shores of the European experience with Socialist and Social Democratic parties.

Even if these considerations did not show that party revitalization and responsibility are impractical solutions to fragmentation, the more recent factors discussed above do. Specifically, the tendency of government growth to erode party incentive systems and the tendency of an issue-conscious upper-middle-class electorate to prefer special-purpose organizations to catchall parties as vehicles of participation will probably remain strong and continue to sap the strength of party contributions and allegiances in the future.

Parties and the New Politics: United States and Europe

Ironically, the hypothesis that at least some partisan decline is to be explained by the accumulation of breakthroughs and their consequences

77. Edward C. Banfield, "In Defense of the American Party System," in Robert A. Goldwin, ed., *Political Parties, U.S.A.* (Rand McNally, 1964), pp. 21–39.

78. Banfield, *Political Influence*.

79. Arthur Schlesinger, Jr., "Crisis of the Party System: I," *Wall Street Journal*, May 10, 1979.

and by changing tastes in modes of political participation among increasingly affluent, mobile electorates draws support from surprisingly similar diagnoses on the European continent, traditionally the home of purposive, responsible parties (though not of "responsible party government" in the British sense). Although these party systems and political structures obviously differ greatly from those in the United States, they share with the United States the progression of welfare state breakthroughs and (partly as a consequence) more affluent, middle-class electorates. In both Europe and the United States, these developments appear to produce a loss or fragmentation of purpose, the growth of rationalizing politics, and a growing incapacity of the parties to define new agendas that inspire mass excitement and elite approval.

Socialists in France and elsewhere, William Pfaff observes, wrestle with the problem of maintaining party spirit now that "the left has won."[80] In today's Europe, Stanley Hoffmann finds that:

> the great ideological "spiritual families" of the past have either disappeared or propose no relevant future. . . . The questions were often either not raised before or were deemed secondary—Will it work? At what costs? Societies that have suffered from the disease of unrestrained ideologies on a rampage . . . now impose a reality test on political visions.[81]

"Ruling," Hoffmann writes, "has become managing."[82]

Suzanne Berger has advanced the thesis that in Western Europe "the new transparencies of the state's impact on daily life and a new perception of the relative autonomy of politics combine with the declining capacity of political institutions to produce a widespread reaction against the state, at the same time that they promote high levels of participation in politics."

80. William Pfaff, "Reflections: The European Left," *The New Yorker*, August 7, 1978, pp. 54–59, quotation at p. 56. In Western Europe, Pfaff writes: "Passionate political controversy takes place over matters that usually amount to very little. Economics dominates the scene, and in the end the argument concerns how certain generally agreed-upon goals can best be achieved. It is really an argument for specialists. The nature of the society sought is not in serious question. . . . The great adventure is over. No one resists Socialism. There is no moral opposition. Socialism has become banal, like democracy: it is possible to argue bitterly about how it should be organized or about the practical priorities of a given moment, but the principle itself is beyond dispute" (pp. 57, 58).

81. Stanley Hoffmann, "Fragments Floating in the Here and Now," *Looking for Europe*, *Daedalus*, vol. 108 (Winter 1979), pp. 1–26, quotations at pp. 17–18.

Guido Goldman observes that in Germany "increasingly, distinctions among the parties have become muted." Ideology has "faded," and "opposition has lost much of its ideological sting." Deep ideological controversy is found mainly within the Social Democratic party, where "left-wing dissidents" challenge moderate leadership, not between the major parties themselves (*The German Political System* [Random House, 1974], pp. 94, 95, 111).

82. Hoffmann, "Fragments," p. 22.

The source of the trend appears to be the multiplication of breakthroughs: "Expanded state intervention . . . led to a politicization of matters that previously were perceived as outside the reach of political solutions." Thus "the issue is not only one of change in the cast of characters; but, equally important, of a vast increase in the number of interactions with the state." Political parties have proved largely unable to contain and capitalize on the numerous discontents with the growing state role; instead, there has occurred a "vast new wave of collective activity outside traditional political institutions," especially "citizens' groups." In consequence, party counts for less in the legislatures and in negotiations with interest groups and the bureaucracy, and intraparty fights make coherent party policies ever more difficult. These developments, Berger writes, "can be found in greater or lesser measure in all of Western Europe." As the catchall parties of both left and right provc unable to transform old ideologies and appeals to fit the demands of a newly affluent Europe and the new realities of the welfare state, bureaucracies and pressure groups tend to gain power, she notes.[83]

The new politics, it appears, are not limited to the United States alone. What has here been taken as their essence and termed rationalizing politics —technocratic, managerial, party-weakening, policy-analytic politics of fragmented principles and eclipsed purposes that depart sharply from widely revered images of the roles of democratic institutions and processes —may be an important component of the postindustrial, post-welfare state politics of the future.

The decline of the political party as a central autonomous policy force points to two important related dangers in the new politics. One is the difficulty of giving institutional expression to the new mass centrism arising from agenda convergence. Another is that the new amateurism accompanying party decline may aggravate endemic weaknesses in American political institutions, diminishing policymaking capability. These dangers, about which one can do little more than speculate, will be briefly discussed in turn.

Parties and the New Centrism

The problems of the political parties in the United States and in Europe bring into clear focus a basic dilemma of the new politics: the new rationalizing mood at once encourages a new centrism and impedes its institution-

83. Suzanne Berger, "Politics and Antipolitics in Western Europe in the Seventies," in *Looking for Europe*, pp. 27–50, quotations at pp. 30, 31, 38, 40, 41, 46.

alization. To mass public and elite alike in both the United States and Europe, big government is now a fact of life, the battles over welfare state breakthroughs largely over. Few would undo the contemporary welfare state, but few trust its benevolence or look with equanimity on its powerful intrinsic forces of growth. Institutionalizing this centrist position is more difficult than arriving at it, however.

Postwar generations that have grown up within big government take it for granted and would not do without it, but nonetheless approach it with a contempt born of familiarity. Both Europe and the United States have in the last thirty years experienced great "middle-classification," both cultural and economic, as a consequence of rising incomes and affluence, higher educational attainment, the spread of mass communication, especially television, and three unbroken decades of peace (at least in Europe) and prosperity.[84] These middle-classifying forces are in a considerable (though unmeasurable) degree the products of the welfare state and the managed economy, that is, of big central government. Yet the same "postmaterialist" values that presuppose the welfare state and are nourished by it call its legitimacy into question.

Improved incomes, education, communication, and general economic and international stability appear to lead to a heightened sense of political efficacy among the "masses," a stronger determination to use politics as a tool of material betterment and of improvements in the quality of life, and greater political distrust, that is, a growing concern with perceived discrepancies between political ideals and official behavior.[85] Education promotes a sense of efficacy—articulateness, a "critical spirit," pride in having opinions—and introduces more and more of the population to political ideas and ideals. The mass media broadcast more frequent and more widespread instances of discrepancies between realities and ideals, increasing distrust. The combination of rising political efficacy, consciousness, and distrust leads in turn to new democratizing demands and especially to demands for greater participation of the rank and file in formal organizations, for a greater say by party members in political parties (triggering challenges to party officialdom), and for a larger role of the average citizen in the general affairs of government (by such means as referenda, devolution, or more closely instructed or monitored representatives).

84. Inglehart, *The Silent Revolution*, chap. 3. This section draws heavily on this source, on Huntington, "Postindustrial Politics," and on Vivien Hart, *Distrust and Democracy* (Cambridge University Press, 1978).

85. Hart, *Distrust and Democracy*, p. 30.

These attitudes have diffused widely throughout society, but they achieve different degrees of depth in different strata. For most of society their effects are shallow and incremental; these groups may be mobilized at times of intense concern, but they mainly remain on the peripheries of politics, where most people stay most of the time. In certain political elites, however—those with the strongest sense of efficacy, consciousness of political duty, and distrust—these attitudes reinforce ideological predispositions and seem to present opportunities for "system transformations." These elites—overlapping circles of the socially, politically, and intellectually concerned and active—play on these themes with a newly broadened potential following that is indeed intermittently attentive and active. This episodic activism confounds both the elites (who may really believe, as did some leftists in the late 1960s and early 1970s, that the revolution is at hand) and critical observers, who denounce the volatility of the electorate and its democratic distempers. No sooner are these apocalyptic predictions advanced, however, than the mobilized lose interest, disperse, and fall back into relative inactivity. Although these episodes do not suffice to create enduring new structures (apart from some special-purpose organizations of varying strengths), they are enough to destabilize existing organizations, parties (the Democratic party in the United States is a prime example), and governments, increasing fragmentation and the sense of public drift.

In time the activist elites, deprived of their temporary mass following, appear to go in different directions. Some make their peace with conventional politics and culture. Some exchange political activism for the counterculture—alternative life-styles, drugs, and the like. Others, however, more politically persistent, try to gain a foothold in the major parties of the left and drive them further leftward. (Where there is no true party of the left, as in the United States, only the first two courses are open to disaffected activists.) Thus electorates that are increasingly centrist, inclined to experiment with ideologies and to pick and choose eclectically among their elements, and even liberal (in the American sense) come to confront parties of the dogmatic, traditional right and leftist parties that are pressured to extremes by ideological cadres.

What happens next depends on the specifics of the country's party system. In Britain the choice between Thatcherite Conservatives and a far left Labour party has created a gap at the center that the new Social Democrats, in coalition with the old Liberals, are moving to fill. In France the Socialists have moved toward the center (and into power), the Communists to the left. In Germany, Helmut Schmidt struggled to keep the Social

Democrats on a steady and moderate left-of-center course but was challenged by the party's left wing, who complained that he was merely another Christian Democrat. Something similar happened in Holland.[86] In Norway, the "left" party was swept from power by "modern" Conservatives preoccupied with tax cuts and balanced budgets but, unlike older Conservatives, accepting of the welfare state.[87] Throughout these cases one sees the efforts of leftist parties to define a modern liberalism (or modern socialism) in hopes of capturing a more centrist electorate. One sees too the problems they face in doing so from small groups of ideological or nontraditional romantic leftists in their own party or coalition or in Communist parties or terrorist cells.

In sum, growing mass centrism is at once a long-term force for political stability and a short-term cause of the breakdown of institutions, especially political parties, whose institutional character necessarily incorporates a large measure of lag, having institutionalized both precontemporary concerns and the deeply held values of entrenched organizational elites. The consolidation of the welfare state and of the managed economy has eroded both the premodern bases of old conservatism and the material and social grievances that nourished old (that is, New Deal-style) liberalism and traditional socialism. The historic agenda of the moderate left has been discharged and institutionalized. Its discharge means that the left now largely lacks a persuasive and extended agenda of its own and must go in search of a new agenda that fits new realities. But the major new reality posing the challenge is, ironically, that its agenda has been institutionalized: the breakthroughs of yesteryear grow with a powerful internal dynamic, uncontrollably. Thus big government finds itself increasingly thrown on the defensive.

In the short term the preoccupation with containing growth of government confers political advantage on the right, which rushes in with its alternatives—retrenchment, deregulation, incentives, and the rest. Once in power, however, conservatives must either temporize and compromise, leaving their regime or party without a distinctive program and their own purist supporters on the far right disillusioned, or persist in implementing doctrinaire programs (for instance, the monetarist attack on inflation) that

86. Andre Spoor, "How Holland's Social Democrats Alienated the Voters," *Wall Street Journal*, May 12, 1982.

87. This account of the 1981 Norwegian election follows Leonard Downie, "Conservatives Favored as Norwegians Vote," *Washington Post*, September 14, 1981; and Downie, "Conservatives Oust Norway's Labor Party," *Washington Post*, September 15, 1981.

produce great suffering, popular discontent, and unease among moderates within the party coalition. Meanwhile the left, bereft of a convincing agenda of its own and embarrassed by the uncontrollability and costs of its programs, must simultaneously move toward the center, generate a rationalizing agenda distinct from and less offensive than that of the confident conservatives, and protect its organizational fabric from the attacks of far left elements, who charge betrayal.

It is difficult to predict where this pressure on old parties to adapt to new political conditions will lead. The major prospects are successful organizational adaptation (perhaps visible in the recent electoral success of a moderate Socialist party in France), the invention of new political organizations (evident in the proliferation of special-purpose groups in the United States and elsewhere and in the creation of Britain's Social Democratic party), and immobilism and drift. What alone is clear is that the choice between "comrades and Christians"[88] (or Labour and Tory) is increasingly unacceptable in Europe, just as the choice between laissez faire Republicanism and New Deal liberalism is no longer satisfactory in the United States.

Parties and the New Amateurism

A second danger in the decline of party in the United States is the loss of the political professional. Despite—indeed to some degree because of—the seemingly technocratic character of many rationalizing issues, the new politics is increasingly conducted by institutional and political amateurs. The trend is evident in all major institutions of American government. Growing centralization of executive powers within the White House means more power for White House staff, officials usually unaccustomed to governmental roles, whose main qualification for their position is long political allegiance to their principal and whose major political experience is in running campaigns. Growth of congressional staff puts increasing influence in the hands of young newcomers to Washington, as does the new reformed Congress, where the activism of junior legislators has expanded rapidly. Efforts to control the bureaucracy by reducing its role in policy initiation augment the roles of generalists at the level of the assistant and deputy assistant secretaries and their staffs, who are often young "idea" men and women, and those of task forces and of roving academic entrepreneurs with

88. The phrase is taken from David I. Kertzer's study of Italian party competition, *Comrades and Christians* (Cambridge University Press, 1980).

ingenious advice but little practical experience. The proliferation of equal rights and general-interest groups opens new opportunities for political influence to young lawyers and other energetic types intent on doing good, wielding power, and making contacts before settling down to a career. Party reform encourages self-appointed candidates to hire a media consultant, get on television, build a personal following, raise money, win a primary, and run on the party line in substantial independence of party leadership. In sum, government is increasingly in the hands of new men and women.

The new amateurs share no common political background or socialization; indeed, they share little beyond their largely upper-middle-class status and outlook, about whose distinctive properties too little is known. These upper-middle-class types do not base their claims to power on such familiar foundations as numbers (as did the working class that ran the old urban political machines and formed the core of the New Deal Democratic coalition); virtue (as did the middle classes with their solid bourgeois sense of moderation, of being in the cultural and economic middle), or birth (as did the upper classes, whose old Americanism gave them a sense of the guardian's special responsibility for the nation's political life). The upper-middle class, by contrast, is a meritocracy: its members got where they did by means of intelligence, articulateness, higher education and the credentials that accompany it, and energy. It is in some respects a nonclass: highly individualistic but socially concerned; entrepreneurial and ambitious but inclined to temper its materialism with a healthy respect for postmaterialist quality-of-life issues; generally principled, but able to see, if not respect, both sides of a question.

The growing political power of the upper-middle-class meritocrats may be an inevitable outgrowth of a basic feature of postindustrial society, namely, "the centrality of theoretical knowledge as the source of innovation and policy analysis in the society."[89] In the past, however, sensitivity and seasoning have been thought to be more important to governing than theoretical knowledge; that the latter can do away with the need for the former is doubtful. As Huntington remarks, "Higher levels of intelligence and knowledge do not necessarily translate into more skillful political judgments and decisions."[90]

One should not overstate the novelty of the amateur politician in the United States. The days of deference politics went out with the Federalists.

89. Bell, *Cultural Contradictions of Capitalism*, p. 198.
90. Huntington, "Postindustrial Politics," p. 190.

A society impressed by the claims of "radical individualism," holding the view that all citizens have equal political capacity, ever eager to maximize citizen participation, and ever distrustful of representatives as usurpers intervening for private advantage between the citizen and his portion of sovereignty, will naturally reserve a large political role for the amateur. In the past, however, stronger party structures, sometimes strong enough to constitute machines, obliged the amateur to cooperate with professionals once the newcomers had successfully fought their way to a share of power. Today the amateurs need neither fight their way to power (except perhaps against each other) nor share it with professionals (increasingly an endangered species) once they have won it.

The simultaneous decline of party professionalism and rise of the amateur impose new stresses on a salient weakness in American policymaking, especially as contrasted with Europe. To be sure, the intermittent American fascination with the disciplined, responsible parties of Europe has been in many ways naive, underestimating the high degree of chaos and even incoherence that can exist within a European party or within a governing coalition.[91] The central difference between American and European parties lies not in the supposed discipline and responsibility of the latter but rather in the protracted, rigorous socialization and apprenticeship that a European party imposes on would-be leaders in their rise to power.[92] High political officials in European government have usually risen through the party ranks over many years of political vocation. In the course of apprenticeship they have watched the party formulate and win acceptance of party positions on the full range of issues before the nation and they have learned the political arts of sustaining the party position, once reached, within an often fractious coalition and against a skilled opposition. American parties have never offered a similar socialization, and today do so less than ever. What is gained in the one case and lost in the other is more readily recognized and appreciated than defined.

91. Alfred Diamant writes: "A simple-minded dichotomy between decentralized U.S. and cohesive European parties will not help much. European political parties, with the possible exception of the communist parties, are not as disciplined and cohesive as their disciplined legislative voting behavior would suggest. Right, center, and left wings can be found in all the socialist and Christian-Democratic parties. . . . Even further loosening up occurs in the presence of coalition governments." "Bureaucracy and Public Policy in Neo-Corporative Settings: Some European Lessons," *Comparative Politics*, vol. 14 (October 1981), p. 113.

92. See Richard Rose, "Government against Sub-governments: A European Perspective on Washington," in Richard Rose and Ezra N. Suleiman, eds., *Presidents and Prime Ministers* (Washington, D.C.: American Enterprise Institute for Public Policy Research, 1980), pp. 284–347, especially pp. 313, 317, 338.

Rationalizing Politics: Opportunities and Strains

The account of rationalizing politics developed here suggests several observations about the new politics and their relation to the national crises of confidence and competence.[93] First, the new politics are not a miscellany of random misfortunes that somehow happened to descend on the United States in the last decade and a half. The new political patterns have a logic and coherence; they are the political products of the evolution of the three great breakthroughs of the last half-century—the U.S. welfare state, the managed economy, and international leadership. They may be traced not to disconnected and accidental or incidental sources, but rather to one major and pervasive source—government growth and the need to cope with it.

Second, if this source of the new politics is acknowledged, it ceases to be satisfying to treat the new trends as dangerous institutional breakdowns born of a combination of naiveté and cynical power plays by imperialist presidents and courts, reform-minded legislators of limited insight, and organizational activists driven by a democratic distemper to seek more participation than the system can tolerate. The changes described here are the handiwork of no such comforting culprits. Their origin lies in more subtle, complex, and powerful forces, in whatever it is that makes government grow—presumably the collective values, preferences, and decisions of the society as a whole, that is, of the American people.

Third, growth of government sets off an institutional chain reaction in which changes in one institution (growth of bureaucracy, for example) put pressures on others to adapt (expanded congressional staff, for instance). Whether these changes are dysfunctional breakdowns or suitable adaptations cannot be judged by inspection of individual institutions uncontaminated by concern for their larger political and interinstitutional context. Political science evaluations, hampered by the disciplinary custom of specializing in the behavior, roles, powers, and functions of discrete institutions, sometimes ignore this point.

Fourth, if the new politics may be traced to the sources found here, much of the railing of academic and journalistic Cassandras against the new patterns is futile. Unfortunately, political scientists have responded to the new politics mainly by trotting out doctrines (administrative responsi-

93. James L. Sundquist, "The Crisis of Competence in Government," in Joseph A. Pechman, ed., *Setting National Priorities: Agenda for the 1980s* (Brookings Institution, 1980), pp. 531–63.

bility, cabinet government, a broad and general legislative oversight role, vital and disciplined parties, and all the rest) against which to denounce centralization in the EOP, the infusion of policy specialists, greater congressional staff, more detailed legislation, greater use of the legislative veto, the growth of administrative rules and regulations, the proliferation of special-interest, single-issue groups, and the decline of party. Readiness to denounce has not always been matched by diligence in carrying out the analyst's first task, understanding and explaining the source of change. The conventional wisdom may represent not (as some appear to think) the eternal principles of political wisdom, but rather the misapplication of old theories to facts they do not fit. There is a need for new political science models capable of analyzing new circumstances, functions, and adaptations in an empirical and dispassionate light.

A fifth consideration is whether the new politics are incapable of addressing major policy problems or are capable only of making them worse. Some would argue that institutional breakdowns, especially party breakdowns, along with the growth of special-purpose groups, must generate increasing fragmentation and a worsening imbalance between severity of policy problems and government's capacity to address them. Terms such as "pluralistic stagnation," "overinstitutionalization," and the "immobility-emergency cycle" have been coined to capture the political incapacity of modern polities.[94]

The distinction between breakthrough and rationalizing politics suggests, however, that the situation is more complex than these terms indicate. In some potential breakthrough arenas—energy policy, for instance —it may well be that pluralism—unconstrained battling among interest groups, citizens' groups, regional interests, and others—will cause policy stagnation. In other arenas, however—national health insurance, for example—group politics are far less important an obstacle than objective doubts about the need for the breakthrough and about the wisdom of enacting it before prior breakthroughs (medicare and medicaid) have been repaired. Indeed, in policy areas subjected to rationalizing politics—health costs, urban aid programs, or transportation regulation, for example—government has been far from stagnant, revising previous arrangements with a speed few would have thought possible ten years ago. Public-sector, ratio-

94. Samuel H. Beer, *British Politics in the Collectivist Age* (Vintage Books, 1969), p. 408; Mark Kesselman, "Overinstitutionalization and Political Constraint: The Case of France," *Comparative Politics*, vol. 3 (October 1970), pp. 21–44; and Karl Deutsch, *Politics and Government: How People Decide Their Fate*, 2d ed. (Houghton Mifflin, 1974), pp. 61–63.

nalizing politics—government's need to generate solutions to government's problems—may prove to be at least a partial antidote to fragmentation and a recurrent source of action. Whether the antidote will be adequate and the actions timely and sensible are questions that lie beyond the scope of this analysis.

The most problematic element in the new politics is not the objective problem-solving capacity of government but the subjective connotations—in a word, government's legitimacy. Various features of the new politics diminish over time government's ability to explain and justify its actions and inactions to its citizens and thereby retain credibility and respect in their eyes.

As several commentators have remarked, the ideological certitudes of the past have been replaced by a contemporary political mood of ambivalence.[95] Government is torn among its wish to do new, bigger, and better things; its awareness that the programs of the past need tedious inspection, repair, and perhaps newly enforced efficiencies and economies; and its uneasy understanding that rationalizing projects challenge, constrain, and hold hostage visions of breakthroughs. Thus, breakthroughs continue to percolate on or near the government's agenda, attracting curiosity and fascination (only made stronger by time and delay) in the media and amid attentive elites, but have a harder time breaking through. The two clearest American examples are national health insurance and a guaranteed annual income: both were annually proclaimed to be imminent, and both failed annually to be enacted, for over a decade. The pattern in sum is institutionalized ambivalence: past breakthroughs are maintained and some are incrementally expanded; new ones are held at or near the horizon; and new programs of management and constraint, often deliberately set at odds with the benefit-conferring breakthroughs, are added to an ever more perplexing policy mix.

It is possible that rationalizing politics will prove to be a temporary phase in U.S. political life, not a more or less permanent condition reached

95. For example, Juan Linz, "Europe's Southern Frontier: Evolving Trends Toward What?" in *Looking for Europe*, pp. 175–209, especially p. 181; Aaron Wildavsky, "Doing Better and Feeling Worse: The Political Pathology of Health Policy," in *Doing Better and Feeling Worse: Health in the United States*, *Daedalus*, vol. 106 (Winter 1977), pp. 105–23, especially p. 122; Lawrence D. Brown, "The Scope and Limits of Equality as a Normative Guide to Federal Health Care Policy," *Public Policy*, vol. 26 (Fall 1978), pp. 481–532, especially pp. 529–32; and Alan I. Abramowitz, "The United States: Political Culture under Stress," in Gabriel A. Almond and Sidney Verba, eds., *The Civic Culture Revisited* (Little, Brown, 1980), pp. 177–211, especially p. 207.

by way of a steady evolution from "pure" breakthrough politics once deadlock had been broken (the Roosevelt and Johnson administrations) to rationalizing breakthroughs (the Nixon years) to a preponderately rationalizing agenda (the Carter and Reagan administrations). Arthur Schlesinger, Jr., for one, predicts that "some time in the eighties the dam will break, as it broke in the sixties, the thirties and at the turn of the century. There will arise a new passion for reform, innovation, experiment and a new opportunity for strong national leadership."[96]

Schlesinger's guesses are better educated than most, but a contrary view is supportable, too. For one thing, indulging these new passions will presuppose solutions to economic problems—lower productivity, high inflation, and a worsening U.S. international economic position, for instance—that may prove more stubborn and less cyclical than American political energies. Second, even if the economy were not a problem, the uncontrollable, self-escalating costs of previous breakthroughs—medicare and social security, in particular—will consume substantial fiscal dividends in the future. And, unless the spirit of Proposition 13 and Reaganomics recedes amid a new passion for taxation, breakthroughs will be hard to finance. Moreover, there seem to be few promising candidates left for future breakthroughs. In many quarters both the need for and feasibility of national health insurance and welfare reform are discounted, and other major fields such as transportation, law enforcement, education, and housing are not likely to be scenes of major new federal commitments soon. Rationalizing politics may be here to stay, at least for the foreseeable future.

One need not entirely despair of this prospect, for the approach is not without attractive features. Above all, it fits the facts. Perhaps the preeminent political fact of the present is that the ideologies that gave order, confidence, and vision to the political thought of attentive elites and average citizens alike—New Deal liberalism, socialism, and conservatism, both libertarian and Burkean—have faltered badly, transparently unable to offer consistently defensible, comprehensive answers to public problems. The resulting tabula rasa is frightening but liberating. A new reasonableness based on acknowledged ambivalence and a due regard for complexity, qualities neglected in more confident days, could be the reward. From a practical standpoint, too, institutionalized ambivalence is today almost surely more prudent and productive of utility on the whole than any more resolute approach.

96. Schlesinger, "Crisis of the Party System."

The problem, however, lies in communicating these points. Politics driven by the courage of our lack of conviction (in playwright Tom Stoppard's words) have no power to stir men's souls and elevate their vision—a good thing or a bad, depending on one's point of view. Moreover, institutionalized ambivalence may be easily mistaken for plain illogic and contradiction. Why should government expand benefits with one hand and constrain them with the other? Why, conservatives wonder, must government add one new, costly program after another—HMOs, PSROs, HSAs, and onward—to correct deficiencies in the design of medicare and private insurance schemes? Why, liberals ask, must national health insurance burn while government fiddles with well-intended but trivial programs like HMOs, PSROs, and HSAs? Having bumped rudely and repeatedly into the limits of its capacity, why cannot government trim its sails and live within limits, conservatives inquire rhetorically, while liberals voice their exasperation that breakthroughs to meet pressing social needs must wait upon arcane rationalizing measures.

Communication is made the more difficult by the nature of the crises politicians face today. From a political standpoint a "good" crisis is one where simple causes seem to be evident for all to see, where simplistic solutions lie near at hand and command consensus, and where the upper and middle classes of the population can identify with efforts to solve someone else's problems. The urban crisis, unpleasant as it was, had these features. Poverty and racism were agreed to be its causes, "wars" on poverty and discrimination the answer, and the warriors and legislators felt good about their exploits. The inflation, energy, and medical cost crises lack all three features (as does crime, which quickly came to replace poverty and deprivation as the heart of the urban crisis). There is little agreement on the relative importance of their several, complex, and interdependent causes; there is little consensus on solutions; and everyone suffers. Urban poverty, Vietnam, and Watergate were viewed at a distance by most of the population. They were moral, not personal, issues. Energy, inflation, and medical costs, by contrast, affect everyone personally and privately. In these areas, analysts are deeply split between those who view too much government as the cause and less government as the answer and those who believe exactly the opposite. Rationalizing politics are painful under these conditions; the political temptation is to pause until consensus develops or to try to steer a middle compromise course. Both responses, of course, displease both camps.

At present, liberal and conservative policymakers lack a lucid and persuasive vocabulary, a new public philosophy adequate to the new politics, that would allow them to explain to their critical ideological brethren outside government why the logical approaches are irresponsible. Government seems condemned to emit signals that are ominously unsettled and unsettling, giving the perpetual impression of (as one prefers) two steps forward and one back or of one forward and two back.

The forces of rationalizing politics appear to be unleashing widespread, deep-seated dissatisfaction with government which may, with Schumpeterian irony, progressively undercut the legitimacy of political institutions themselves. Five sources of delegitimation are of major importance, each of them nourished by the basic components of rationalizing politics. First, as the number of interactions between government and interest groups multiplies, the pitch and frequency of interest group complaints about the arbitrariness and irrationality of government increase, too. The torrent of objections to governmental regulation is the clearest current case in point. Second, the sustained disaffection of single-issue citizens' groups over government's inability or unwillingness to realize more of their agenda more quickly produces another countervailing string of righteous critiques. Even as business groups attack government overregulation of the environment, product contents, and worker-safety conditions, public interest lobbies complain that government, captured by business, does too little in these fields. The most powerful convergence of recent years, as Berger observes of Western Europe, is the convergence of both left and right on vociferous antistatism.

Third, a larger governmental role inevitably means increased bureaucratic interaction with more of the citizenry. For reasons explored above, these contacts generate friction and tension on a larger scale and contribute to the ever simmering antibureaucratic mood of the citizenry. That the bureaucracy is an attractive target for producer groups, public interest groups, and politicians alike greatly increases the chorus of complaint, of course. Fourth, as the growth of government and its halting efforts at self-repair give muckraking television and newspaper reporters ever larger quantities of muck to rake, the increasingly literate, educated, opinionated, and attentive middle and upper-middle classes are increasingly deluged with evidence of the imprudence and unwisdom of their political leaders. Fifth, as policy analysts in the academic community come increasingly into contact with policymakers, offer their advice, and see it disregarded, watered down, or misapplied, they add their voices to the general cry that government is irrational and perverse. The reasons why their scenarios and modules cannot or should not be adopted intact in the real world are obviously of less interest to these analysts than the fact that government defeated the wisdom it showed in soliciting their advice by somehow botching the job of implementing it. If the antigovernmental rhetoric from these five sources persists and builds, as it almost surely will, it cannot fail to undercut popular confidence in government, perhaps seriously.

The last three decades have produced important changes in the interplay between politics and policy. The frustration of the deadlock-breakthrough syndrome (the 1950s and early 1960s) was supplanted by a heady interval of triumphant and seemingly limitless breakthroughs (the middle and late 1960s), which then gave way in the 1970s to the disappointments of ever imminent breakthroughs held hostage to a technocratic politics of fragmented and limited purposes and absorbed in the malfunctions of the past. Over time, government and society have separated: public-sector politics at a substantial remove from constituency forces give Washington the appearance of isolation, and the antagonism of attentive elites gives government the aura of incompetence.

In the new conditions of rationalizing politics, the time-honored and hitherto-prized American determination to steer a middle course, acceptable on the whole to a majority of the population, ends by antagonizing a citizenry that recognizes complexity and ambivalence but looks to government to cut through complexities, not lament them, and to resolve ambivalence, not institutionalize it. For good and sufficient reasons, government declines to take the steps needed truly to rationalize its policies. "True" rationality—reductions of government entitlements, experiments with incentives on a large scale, extensive deregulation, regulation, reorganization, and planning—requires uncertain steps and costs and is certain only to involve major dislocations and pain, both political and social.

The problem is an old and familiar one: although everyone has a preferred list of programs to be eliminated, rationalized, or expanded, a consensus on what ought to be done does not automatically result from assembling the lists. Discontents are additive; programmatic mandates are not.[97]

97. As Herbert Kaufman remarks in a related connection: "Even if everybody agreed in principle that terminating government programs was the best way to reduce red tape, experience indicates that each interest group construes this blanket policy to include only the programs that it cares little or nothing about, not the programs from which it benefits directly. Remote activities are expendable; those that hit close to home are indispensable. In these circumstances, the inevitable outcome is logrolling. Groups join in the defense of things to which they are indifferent in order to win allies for the things they are really concerned about. In the end, practically nothing will disappear" (*Red Tape*, p. 67).

Policymakers therefore experiment with halfway measures that enjoy broad but shallow support, and, not surprisingly, these tentative measures prove unequal to solving the problems they address. In the meantime, incremental or self-generated extensions of benefits aggravate problems, making the rationalizing programs work harder, yet they fail to appease those who wonder why true breakthroughs or true efficiency must take a back seat to measures whose unworkability can be explained in a few crisp sentences by any columnist or professor.

Policymakers, in short, continue to apply the famous political logic of the bell-shaped curve, pursuing policies which they intuitively feel are broadly if not fully acceptable to the mainstream of the population. Alas, they now apply this logic to a population increasingly fragmented between centrist masses and principled elites that are increasingly issue conscious, single-issue organized, unsympathetic with aggregation and compromise, and out of sorts with government altogether. These frictions may be irreducible. A highly decentralized political system, one bound to share power among three coequal branches of government at three levels of a federal system and determined to divide social power between the public and private sectors, must inevitably aggregate, compromise, obscure, split differences, and institutionalize ambivalence, if it is to act and govern at all, let alone well. This proposition deserves more attention than political analysts have seen fit to give it of late. Until the critical constituencies and elites recognize that U.S. political structures set important limits on what political action can accomplish, that these structures must always retain the ambivalent character of treasured inheritance and damned nuisance, the new politics may remain the nation's preeminent argument for nostalgia.